W9-COT-599

A Handbook of Christian Latin : Style, Morphology, and Syntax

A Handbook of Christian Latin : Style, Morphology, and Syntax

by Albert Blaise

Translated by
Grant C. Roti

BREPOLS

Georgetown University Press, Washington, D.C.

For Linda, Arthur, and Kristin

Library of Congress Cataloging-in-Publication Data

Blaise, Albert. 1894-
[Manuel du latin chrétien. English]
A handbook of Christian Latin: style, morphology, and syntax / by Albert Blaise; translated by Grant C. Roti.
176 p. 24,5 x 15,5 cm.
Includes index.
ISBN 0-87840-237-3 (paper)

1. Latin language, Postclassical - Grammar. 2. Christian literature. Early-Latin authors - History and criticism. 3. Latin language. Postclassical - Style. I. Title.

PA2306.B4 1992 477-dc20 92-20995 CIP

Printed in Belgium
D/1994/0095/17
ISBN 2-503-50371-3
U.S. ISBN 0-87840-237-3

Contents

Translator's Preface

Albert Blaise first published his *Manuel du latin chrétien* in 1955. As he mentions in his preface, it was originally intended to be an introduction for his *Dictionnaire latin-français des auteurs chrétiens* (Turnhout, Belgium: Brepols, 1954) but was eventually published as a separate work. Hence all abbreviations used in citations in the *Manuel* can be found in the front matter of that dictionary, and all references by Blaise to 'the dictionary' refer to that work. The *Manuel* was reprinted in 1986 with a foreword by the publisher and without the original bibliography since a new, updated bibliography was in preparation by G. Sanders and M. Van Uytfaughe. This bibliography was published in 1989 by Brepols, under the title *Bibliographie signalétique du Latin des Chrétians*, as Vol. I of the *Lingua Patrum* subseries of the *Corpus Christianorum* series. (The new copy of the 1986 *Manual* which I purchased also contained handwritten corrections.)

One of the difficulties in translating a work of this sort is that French grammarians have some grammatical concepts which are slightly different from English and American concepts, for example, the French *complément d'objet* may refer to an English and American 'direct object', 'indirect object', or 'objective complement'. For the user of this translation, these differences will pose no practical problems at all; but, here and there throughout the translation, I have included the French terms in brackets for those scholars who may be familiar with French concepts and would appreciate knowing the precise concept which is being translated. Beginning students can safely ignore the French terminology in square brackets. For my understanding of French grammatical terms I depended on Jean-Claude Chevalier, et al., *Grammaire Larousse du français contemporain* (Paris: Libraire Larousse, 1964).

As for the English grammatical terminology, I have tried to be as traditional as possible, drawing upon the following works: Randolph Quirk, et al., *A Grammar of Contemporary English* (New York: Seminar Press, 1972) and *A Comprehensive Grammar of the English Language* (London: Longman, 1985); George O. Curme, *Parts of Speech and Accidence* (Boston: D.C. Heath, 1935), *Syntax* (Boston: D.C. Heath, 1931), and *English Grammar*, Barnes and Noble College Outline Series (New York: Barnes and Noble, 1947); and John E.

Warriner, *English Grammar and Composition*, Complete Course, Franklin Edition (New York: Harcourt Brace and Jovanovich, 1982).

The Latin grammars that I have used and to which I have referred are listed in the Abbreviations.

I have retained exactly the section numbering of the original; the rest of Blaise's labyrinthine numbering system has been followed closely but not always exactly.

All comments in square brackets are mine.

I have silently made corrections of obvious typographical errors in Blaise (for example, in footnote 30 of this translation δέ has been changed to δὲ), but a few corrections should be mentioned:

on p. 9 of this translation Blaise's *incorruptionen* and *immortalitaten* have been changed to *incorruptionem* and *immortalitatem*;
on p. 10 *si Christus persona Paterni spiritus est, Praescr. 14* has been changed to *Ergo si Christus persona Paterni Spiritus est,* TERT. *Prax. 14 (ed. Kr.)* in accordance with the correction made by Blaise in the Addenda and Corrigenda of his *Dictionnaire latin-français des auteurs chrétiens*, p. 899.
on p. 11 *caput uiri mulier* has been changed to *caput autem mulieris, uir est.*
on p. 32 a comma has been added after *earth*;
on p. 56 *particularité* has been read and translated as *particulars*;
on p. 59 *redderre* has been changed to *reddere*;
on p. 64 αὐτοὔς has been changed to αὐτούς;
on p. 82 *Io. 3 Ep. 3, 10* has been changed to *Io. 3 Ep. 1, 13*;
on p. 98 *chap.* has been read and translated as *section*;
on p. 100 *parce* has been read and translated as *because*;
on p. 121 αὐτοῦς has been changed to αὐτούς;
in footnote 6, p. 5, *suffixes* has been changed to *prefixes*, which seems to be what Blaise had in mind;
in footnote 12, p. 14, *dispondaïque* (the French form) has been changed to *dispondaicus* (the Latin form).

Four changes have been made in the Index:

on p. 149 *Les chiffres renvoient aux paragraphs* has been translated *Numbers refer to sections*:
on p. 151 *Dum « tandis que »* has been translated Dum, 'whereas' and the number 301 has been changed to 300;
on p. 155 *Quando, 'alors que pourtant'* has been translated as *[Quando] 'when'*, omitting *pourtant.*
on p. 156 *Subordination (conjunctions de) introduisant le discourse direct* has been translated changing *direct* to *indirect.*

Four people deserve special thanks: Gary Meltzer, who scrupulously analyzed and discussed numerous Greek passages with me; Helen Burke, who proofread the entire manuscript, correcting my English, Blaise's French, and the Latin citations; Jacqueline de la Chapelle-Skubly, without whose constant assistance and encouragement the work would not have been done at all; and Father Richard J. O'Brien of the Linguistics Department, Georgetown University, who painstakingly edited and composed the text for Georgetown University Press.

Thanks also to my wife, Linda, who endured and kept order; my son, Arthur, who listened to and proofread the Latin citations with me; and my daughter, Kristin, who made the whole thing seem like a thrilling event.

Grant C. Roti
28 December 1993

Foreword [of 1986 reprint of French edition]

This little book by Albert Blaise has already performed a great service for all who are interested in Christian Latin literature.

The reader who is familiar only with Classical Latin feels helpless in the presence of certain forms, certain expressions, and certain grammatical anomalies which seem to him incorrect, even aberrant.

The *Handbook of Christian Latin*, making no pretense of erudition, follows step by step classical stylistics and grammar, describing succinctly the characteristics of Christian Latin in the many phases of its evolution and its divergence from classical usage. This practical method has proved its usefulness; the numerous, repeated demands for the book since the depletion of the first printing are evidence of this.

Editions Brepols, which already publishes the *Dictionnaire latin-français des auteurs chrétiens* by Albert Blaise (1st ed., Strasbourg, 1954; 2nd ed., Turnhout, 1967) and his *Dictionnaire latin-français du moyen-âge* (Turnhout, 1975), has decided to reprint, just as it is, the *Handbook of Christian Latin* by the same author. However, the bibliography appended to the 1955 edition, being for the most part out-of-date, has not been reprinted; but an exhaustive bibliography of information on the language of the Christian writers of antiquity and of the early Middle Ages has been in preparation for some time by Professors G. Sanders and M. Van Uytfanghe of the University of Ghent. This bibliography will be published separately as an introductory volume to the new series of Editions Brepols entitled *Lingua Patrum*. In the meantime the unpretentious *Handbook* by the inexhaustible researcher Albert Blaise will remain a reliable and precise guide for the reader of the Latin Fathers.

Preface [to original French edition, 1955]

The contents of this work were originally intended to serve as an introduction to the *Dictionnaire latin-français des auteurs chrétiens*, but it seemed to us that a handbook of this kind, published separately, would be more helpful and would be, in any case, more accessible.

In contrast to the *Dictionnaire*, which extends its investigations to the end of the Merovingian period, only examples taken from the Patristic period, properly speaking, will be mentioned here (with some very rare exceptions).

After a brief explanation of the stylistics of Christian writers, we set forth a series of grammatical 'observations'. There is no question then of this being a theoretical study of Christian Latin, something like a continuation of the history of the Latin language; in fact, I do not foresee the completion of a work of that kind in the near future. Instead, one has available today numerous monographs where the principle grammatical characteristics peculiar to Late Latin have been fully and nicely explained. The task we set for ourselves was to compare these characteristics with our readings and to arrange them within the traditional framework of our Latin grammars. Indeed, all students now study Latin starting from the time of the classical writers; so it is by referring to classical usage that the reader will find here what is at variance with it. This information, set out in this way, will look like a mere catalogue of anomalies, a convenient catalogue, however, for whoever has to read the Christian writers without much practice in the language. But let there be no misunderstanding; the stylistic considerations which form the first part of this handbook will have shown, I hope, that the life of Christian Latin does not reside in this grammatical scheme.

Also, we could not avoid appearing to put on the same level some generally acccepted uses of the language and some rarities peculiar to second-rate writers; to make distinctions would have required many annoying notes and references at the bottom of the page. The difference in the characteristics of the language will mitigate this inconvenience, as much as possible. Furthermore, the reader will be informed by the references, and if a grammatical characteristic is attested only in the *Peregrinatio Aetheriae*, for example, it will not occur to him to give it the same importance that it commands in the work of Saint Augustine.

Since it pertains to the preface, let me make this observation: Christian writers,* like their contemporaries, received, with a few exceptions, a school training in which the classical tradition was always very much alive; I had only to indicate the departures from Classical Latin, not the conformity to it. Grouped together, these departures appear more important than they are in the actual texts where they are often drowned in a more traditional context. One final remark in conclusion: I use *Late Latin* [*latin tardif*] just as a foreigner uses *later Latin* in English or *Spätlatein* in German. At the beginning of the Syntax I explain what must be understood by the term *decadent* in the area of grammar. As to the term *Low Latin*, which has a pejorative connotation, it would without a doubt be suitable for certain texts of popular origin or of the Merovingian period; but to apply it indiscriminately to the great writers of the last centuries of the Empire is to create a dangerous confusion.

—*Albert Blaise*

---

* For references to writers, the reader should consult the 'Liste des auteurs et des ouvrages cités', published at the front of my *Dictionnaire latin-français des auteurs chrétiens*. [See Appendix 2 for a selection from this 'Liste'.]

ERRATA

P. ix, line 11: "Chrétians" should read "Chrétiens".
P. 77, line 15: "rubus" should read "rebus".
P. 78, line 20: "objective" should read "object".
P. 86, line 17: "can be replaced by" should read "can replace".
P. 88, line 11: "how" should read "why".
P. 90, line 33: "It is" should read "They are".
P. 95, line 29: "semitipsum" should read "semetipsum".
P. 143, line 11: "Ep. 22 and 22" should read "Ep. 22 and 23".
P. 157, line 9: "provided that ... that" should read "provided that ... not".

ABBREVIATIONS

Grammars are referred to by section numbers.

AG = *Allen and Greenough's New Latin Grammar.* Ed. J.B. Greenough, G.L. Kittredge, A.A. Howard, and Benjamin L. D'Ooge. Boston: Ginn and Co., 1916.

GL = Gildersleeve, B.L., and Gonzalez Lodge. *Latin Grammar.* 3rd ed. London: MacMillan, 1895.

L = Lane, George M. *A Latin Grammar for Schools and Colleges.* 1903. New York: AMS Press, 1970.

ap. = *apud* (in the writings of)
c. = *columna* (column)
in. = *initio* (at the beginning)
pr. = *praefatione* [?] (in the preface)
praef. = *praefatione* (in the preface)
prol. = *prologo* (in the prologue)
var. = variant reading

§§ = a section containing uncommon grammatical characteristics (see footnote 23, p. 44)

Part One: The Christian style

The Latin of the Christian writers

§1 Our dictionaries speak of Ecclesiastical Latin, the Latin of the Church. The dissertations published by the Catholic University of Washington, D.C., also use the expression *Ecclesiastical Latin.* Goelzer, however, in the preface to his Latin-French dictionary (1st ed., 1892) was already speaking about the 'Christian Latin language'. As for Mgr. Schrijnen, he distinguished '*Kirchlatein*' from '*Christlatein*', 'Church Latin' from 'Christian Latin'.[1] Indeed, it would be more exact and precise to call the terms peculiar to theology, to canon law, to the history of the liturgy—to call these terms *Ecclesiastical Latin* whereas the expression *Christian Latin* would indicate in a more general way the Latin of Christian writers in so far as it has been renewed and transformed by the Christian mentality. It is not difficult to point out some new terms, such as *baptismus, episcopus*, and *saluator*, and some new meanings, as in *peccatum* and *communio.* Ecclesiastical Latin is composed of technical terms, one might say, pertaining either to theology, such as *contritio, trinitas*, and *impeccantia*; or to the liturgy, such as *palla, matutina*, and *missa*; or to canon law, such as *incardinatio, incardinare*, and *canonicus.* But, when we speak of Christian Latin, we are taking into account a more profound originality.

§2 Of what does this originality consist? It is a rather delicate question. Since the first works of Roensch and Goelzer, scholars had begun to focus more and more on the vocabulary of Christian writers. A publication like *Archiv für lateinische Lexicographie*, inaugurated in 1884, devoted considerable space to Christian Latin. Yet immediately after its appearance, the originality of Christian Latin was contested: 'ein eigentliches Kirchenlatein gibt es überhaupt nicht,' [there is no actual Ecclesiastical Latin at all] Karl Sittl categorically declared in the very publication just mentioned (in the year 1884, p. 282). So

---

[1] *Charakteristik des altchristlichen Latein* (Nijmegen, 1932). This work inaugurated the series of publications which is mentioned later.

also today Miss Mohrmann[2] has not drawn to her point of view the votes of all Latinists, and many refuse to regard the Latin of Christian writers as a special language.

Let me remark, first of all, that the expression *Christian Latin* is a short and convenient expression, whatever the reality that lies behind it. At first sight, this reality is rather complex: it is a matter of writers and historical periods which are so diverse! Moreover, my intention and role, in this handbook and even more so in the dictionary itself, is not to formulate a theory but to set forth the facts.

The first is this: the least experienced Latinist, if he puts aside a secular writer to undertake the reading of a Christian writer, feels himself plunged into a new world. A new world of ideas and feelings, of course; but he also has the impression that the language itself has been transformed, or is a new language.

§3 I shall try later to be more precise about this impression by showing that Christian Latin is characterized by its predilection for a figurative style and particularly by the warmer emotional quality of its vocabulary.

Let me admit beforehand that the originality of Christian Latin would be difficult to find in the area of grammar. We obviously move away from Classical Latin; but the facts that we point out in our 'observations,' aside from a certain number of Hellenisms[3] introduced by the translations of the Bible or of the Greek Fathers, as well as some Hebraisms, appear also in the non-Christian writers of the Late Empire. The remarks of a specialist of Late Latin like Löfstedt are based on citations taken from the pagan writers as well as the Christian.

§4 This does not in any way disparage the significance of studies like those which have been published in Washington, D.C., in the collection called *Patristic Studies*, where the grammatical characteristics are studied as much as the semantic. We have all the more reason to acknowledge that the publications of the school of Nijmegen often produce genuine discoveries. This school is more interested in research on style and vocabulary. Scholars there have gotten into the habit of distinguishing particularly (in Christian Latin) 'mediate Christianisms', terms peculiar to Christians for expressing some common ideas, and 'immediate Christianisms', terms expressing specifically Christian ideas.

---

[2] The Bibliography lists works published by the school of Nijmegen, *Latinitas christianorum primaeua*, under the names of Schrijnen, Mohrmann, Janssen, Merkx, et al. For the discussions aroused by the question of Christian Latin, the reader can consult the *Revue des Études latines* of the years 1932, 1936, 1938, and 1940 as well as the articles of P. de Ghellinck in *Les Études classiques* of the years 1939 and 1944.

[3] Before Christian Latin literature proper appeared, Christian texts written in Greek were being translated into Latin in the course of the second century: the *Bible*, the *Epistle of Clement to the Corinthians*, and the *Shepherd of Hermas*; and in the following centuries translated texts hold an important place in Western Latin. On this subject, see the articles or the works of Bardy and Mohrmann mentioned in the bibliography.

Unfortunately, until now the dictionaries have profited little from this progress. If one excepts, of course, the *Thesaurus*[4] (far indeed from being finished—and not everyone has a copy within reach), our dictionaries, even the more voluminous ones, are rather deficient in regard to Christian Latin. For the language of the fourth, fifth, and sixth centuries the translations are often approximate or, frankly, erroneous. The new meanings are rarely mentioned. Many of the terms are missing; and yet they should have as much right to be quoted in a Latin dictionary as those words religiously collected in Festus or in the old glossaries, and as much right as those words that one never encounters in a writer—words which unnecessarily fill up even works intended for scholarly purposes.

---

[4] And also Souter, *A Glossary of Later Latin* (Oxford, 1949), which contains a large part of the Christian vocabulary but gives only some references, without citations.

1 Vocabulary

1 Word formation

§5 The works devoted to the Latinity of a particular Christian writer have shown the abundance of terms derived from Greek by Christian writers, the great number of words that they have created or the neologisms that they have adopted and circulated widely (but these works have not thoroughly examined the meanings of the terms). Let us review the classifications that are reproduced in an almost identical way in a hundred works:

terms derived from Greek: *catholicus, diaconus, eleemosyna*[5];
nouns formed with the aid of the suffixes *-tas, -tio, -io, -sio, -ium, -tor, -atus, -arius, -tura, -tus, -sus, -tia, -ela, -men, -mentum, -icum*;
adjectives with *-bilis, -alis, -aris, -arius, -orius, -torius, -eus, -ius, -iuus, -anus, -osus*;
adverbs with *-ter, -e*;
verbs with *-scere, -ficare* (the last are very frequent in Christian Latin, as are their derivatives in *-ficatio, -ficator, -trix*);
verbs derived from adjectives: *captiuare*;
verbs derived from nouns: *prophetare*;
verbs composed of two words: *benedicere, benesentire*;
numerous compound adverbs or prepositions: *abante, desuper*;

[5] Miss Mohrmann (*Traits caractéristiques...*, see Bibliography) points out that these Greek terms have been preserved in general for concrete things, i.e. the institutions and the hierarchy, whereas the Christian language has used the Latin words and given them a new meaning when it was a matter of expressing abstract or spiritual ideas, like redemption or salvation.

numerous compounds formed with a preposition,[6] especially *cum, in, prae, super*; and even with two prepositions: *subintrare, superextollere*;
compounds with *archi-, pseudo-*, much more numerous than in Classical Latin;
compounds, adjective + noun, designed to translate certain Greek words: *uniformis* (μονοειδῆς);
they are sometimes written as two words: *Deo amabilis* (θεοφιλῆς);
diminutive numbers, especially with *-ulus*;
the use of diminutives of Classical Latin with the sense of the root word: *auricula, apicula.*

Thus most of the derivatives and compounds have been formed according to the Latin tradition. But Classical Latin was certainly more fastidious when it was a matter of admitting a word not established by usage; the Christians, like other writers of their time, used a method without restrictions or scruples. The only ones to sometimes tell us of their hesitations are the most educated writers, such as St. Augustine or St. Jerome.

2 Stylistics[7]

§6 **2.1** Adverbs, placed immediately after or before a noun, can have the meaning of an adjective, in imitation of the Greek, which in this case places the adverb between the article and the noun:

principes semper Africae, TERT. Pall. 1, 'the African princes of all times';
retro dignitas, Cult. fem. 2, 9, 'former dignity';
semper regnum, CYPR. Zel. 18;
uere martyres, Ep. 37, 4;
illi quondam gigantes, SALV. Gub. 6, 23;
locum quondam Benedicti, CASS., Var. 1, 36, 'the place of the deceased Benedict (of days gone by, ancient)';
ciconia redeuntis anni iugiter nuntiatrix, Var. 2, 14, 'continual messenger of spring'.

§§ This practice is rare in Classical Latin: *omnes undique parricidae*, SALL. Cat. 14.

Notice the analogous use of adverbial modifiers [*compléments circonstanciels*] with a noun, rare in Classical Latin:

---

[6] Certain compound words have the same meaning as the root verb, e.g. *constupesco* = *stupesco*. Inversely, a great number of simple verbs are found that have the meaning of the compound, e.g. *ponere* for *deponere*, *firmare* for *affirmare*, *tenere* for *retinere*. The dictionary will inform us about the confusion of prefixes: *dimitto, demitto; abripio, adripio; praeuideo, prouideo; etc.*

[7] With the traditional meaning, as in Berger, *Stylistique latine* (Klincksieck); we later use the same word with another meaning.

pro ueritate contumelia, GREG.-M. Moral. 10, 16, 'insults suffered for truth';
Spiritus Sancti super eum mansio, PS.-CYPR. Rebapt. 8;
episcoporum in Africa numerus, CYPR. Ep. 55, 6.

In the following example, *bene uenisti*, PASS. PERP. 4, 'you are welcome', the adverb has the force of a predicate adjective. And in this other example, *opto meis bene*, CASS. Var. 12, 5, it replaces a noun. This use of *bene* belongs to Vulgar Latin; Plautus earlier supplied analogous examples.

§7 **2.2** From the beginning of the Latin language, certain words, such as *amicus, inimicus, affinis, etc.*, could be categorized as nouns or adjectives. During the Empire, a great number of adjectives and participles are used as nouns, and in Late Latin this use develops further:

2.2.1 Adjectives in the singular, *leprosus, paralyticus, uiolentus, laicus, gentilis, haereticus, etc.*; and, while speaking of the devil, *aduersarius, malignus*; in the neuter: *medium* 'the middle', *salutare* 'salvation', *hibernum* 'winter', even with a noun modifying it [*complément de nom*]:

ad sublime gratiae caelestis, AMBR. Psal. 45, 18;
in medio aluei IORD. Get. 30, 158 (= in medio alueo);

§8 **2.2.2** Adjectives in the plural: *increduli, luxuriosi, gentiles, catholici, etc.*; in the neuter: *caelestia, terrena, carnalia, spiritalia, etc.*; *debilia*, GREG.-M. Moral. 2, 1; *fortia*, COMM. Apol. 40, 'forces'; even with a noun modifying it [*complément de nom*] (which is found only among the poets in Classical Latin):

propter incerta exitus, AMBR. Psal. 1, 16;
praerupta terrarum, VICT.-VIT. 1, 3;
dulcia diuini eloquii, CASS. Psal. c. 12D;
per diuersa regionum, LACT. Inst. 4, 27, 17;

§9 **2.2.3** Present participles,[8] generally in the plural, e.g. *credentes* 'believers', *diffidentes* 'the unbelievers', *discentes* 'catechumens', *etc.*

nolumus autem uos ignorare de dormientibus, VVLG. 1 Thess. 4, 12, 'we do not want you to be ignorant of what concerns the dead';

even when the participle has a modifier or a modifying phrase [*complément*], *consueuerat euntes ad Antonium ducere*, HIER. Vit. Hil. 30, 'he used to guide visitors to Antony' (in Classical Latin, such a participle was rarely used apart from those cases in which it had an antecedent expressed or understood);

---

[8] Rarely some future participles, e.g. *ingressuros baptismum...orare oportet*, TERT. Bapt. 20 (in a general sense: 'those who want to be baptized', those who later will be called *competentes*).

§10 **2.2.4** Past participles in the singular or in the plural, *collecta* 'final prayer', *relicta* 'widow', *dilecta, offensa, etc.*; *incensum, statutum, etc.*; *praepositi* 'the leaders', *lapsi* 'those who have fallen away, the apostates', *etc.*

§11 **2.3** Many gerundives were used as descriptive adjectives, *abominandus, adorandus, fugiendus, laudandus, dolendus, mirandus, miserandus, reuerendus, uenerandus,*[9] *etc.*; or as nouns, *agenda, legenda, etc.*

§12 **2.4** Inversely, some nouns are used as adjectives:
peccator populus, CYPR. Dom. orat. 10;
gentes apostatrices, VVLG. Ez. 2, 3;
accusatrix cogitatio, AVG. Serm. 351, 7.

§13 **2.5** The use of the adjective in lieu of the genitive of possession was already developed in Old Latin, as well as in the poets (*Aeneia nutrix*, VIRG. Aen. 7, 1); in Late Latin, the adjective is encountered almost exclusively with words like *femineus, tyrannicus, angelicus, dominicus.* The last is very frequent:
Dominica indignatio, VVLG. Ier. 23, 19, 'the indignation of the Lord';
Dominica praecepta, TERT. Paen. 3;
Dominica caro, Carn. Chr. 6;
cf. Ariana rabies, HIER. Ep. 16, 2, 'the madness of Arius'.

Inversely, in the chapter on the genitive it will be found that this case is used in place of the adjective.

§14 **2.6** The neuter adjective, in the singular or the plural, used in the adverbial sense by the poets, becomes common in the prose writers of our period, *incerta reptant*, TERT. Paen. 6.

§§ Sometimes the adjective is used with the force of an intensive adverb: *uallem...ingens planissimam*, PEREG. 1, 1, 'immensely large' (Vulgar Latin). (See Syntax, chapter 3, 5.2.)

§15 In imitation of the Greek, one finds predicate adjectives of the subject, in lieu of an adverb:
superueniat...repentina dies illa, VVLG. Luc. 21, 34, (ἐπιστῇ αἰφνίδιος).
domum matutinus ascendit, RVF. Hist. 10, p. 963, 26.

This use, which is found earlier in Vergil, Livy, and Tacitus, becomes frequent in Christian Latin translations and in writers like Fulgentius, Cassian, Victor Vitensis, Saint Benedict, and Boethius.

---

[9] In the superlative, *desideratissimus* and *desiderantissimus* came to be used indifferently, undoubtedly by confusion of the present participle with the gerundive.

§16 **2.7** We must note especially an extraordinary development of the use of abstract words:

2.7.1 In place of a personal pronoun:

cum tua grauitate ac sapientia conferre, CYPR. Ep. 72, 1;
obsecro te ignoscas tarditati meae, HIER. Ep. 99, 2;
disparatus a uestro consortio, LIBER. ap. LVCIF. p. 320, 23;
uestram sanctitatem, CONC. S. I, 2, p. 39, 18 (ὁσιότητα).

This is a part of epistolary etiquette, and we later refer to numerous salutations in letters and to the most varied polite formulas in Augustine, Paulinus of Nola, Gregory the Great, and others. Likewise in the sermons, the religious orator does not say simply *fratres* but:

uestra fraternitas, LEO-M. Serm. 19, 1;
fraterna sanctitas uestra, AVG. Enarr. psal. 2, 5;
sanctitas uestra, ibid. 25, 2, 1.

§17 **2.7.2** In place of a concrete noun either in the singular in a collective sense:

captiuitatem reducere, VVLG. Deut. 30, 3, 'to take back the captives'; cf. AVG. Catech. 21, 37;
nos enim sumus circumcisio, VVLG. Philipp. 3, 3, 'we are the true circumcised';
fraternitas, CYPR. Ep. 5, 7; HIER. Ep. 85, 3; TERT.; Marc. 5, 4, 'brothers, the Church';
transmigratio, VVLG. Dan. 2, 25, 'the exiles';

and often in a non-collective sense:

istam foedare iuuentam, PS.-CYPR. Sodom. 43, 'to sully that youthfulness, that young woman';
omni uilitate uel extremitate contentus, BEN. Reg. 7;
immolatio, HIER. Ez. hom. 7, 10; AVG. Ep. 36, 30, 'victim';
mare et plenitudo eius, VVLG. Ps. 95, 11, 'the sea and all that it contains';
misericordia, CYPR. Op. et al. 4; SALV. Eccl. 2, 1, 'alms';

or very frequently in the plural, *affectiones* 'affections', *amaritudines* 'offenses', *uoluntates* 'acts of the will', *etc.*

§18 **2.7.3** With a phrase modifying it [*complément de nom*], the abstract word is equivalent to a participle:

amissio ciuium, TERT. Apol. 37 = amissi ciues; cf. caesionum cateruae Apol. 31 [? perhaps *in caesionum cateruas*, Apol. 39], 'a band of brawlers';

or is equivalent to an adjective:

ueritas pietatis, FILASTR. 109, 7 = uera pietas;
uoti libertate se obstringere, AVG. Vid. 5, 6, 'to bind oneself by a free vow';
superbia Iudaeorum, Serm. 185, 2 = Iudaei superbi;

cilicii asperitate uelati, CASSIAN. Inst. 1, 2, 4.

§19 **2.7.4** It can also replace a verb (cf. *cognitionem habent faciliorem*, CIC. Fin. 5, 12, 34, 'are easier to understand'):

stationem imperauit soli et lunae, HIER. Iou. 2, 15, 'he ordered the sun and the moon to stand still';
ad innocentiae suae commendationem, TERT. Apol. 2, 'for proving their innocence';
exspectant resurrectionem et ad dextram collocationem, AVG. Vrb. 1, '...and to be placed on the right';
caritas...est tenacitas et firmitas unitatis, CYPR. Bon. pat. 15, 'love supports and strengthens the unity'.

§20 **2.8** Even nouns ending in *-tor* can replace a verb:

nec iam reuelator ipse erit, TERT. Marc. 4, 25, 'will not to be able to reveal';
quaerit intellectorem, AVG. Serm. 252 in., 'needs to be explained';
luminis imperator, PS.-AVG. Serm. 157, 1, 'he who has governed the light';
extitit supplicator tantum ut..., IORD. Get. 52, 271, 'he begged in such a way that...'(cf. simulator et dissimulator, SALL. Cat. 5).

§21 **2.9** Some concrete nouns have acquired an abstract meaning,[10] *compages* 'unity, mystical bond' (*ipsi autem non sunt in illa ecclesiae compage*, AVG. C. litt. Petil. 2, 108, 247).

Most of the new meanings introduced by Christian Latin have been created precisely to give an abstract connotation to terms which until then referred only to concrete realities; we shall say more about them later.

§22 **2.10** Some abstract nouns are objects [*compléments*] of verbs which are normally constructed with an object that has a concrete meaning (Hebraic style):

uestire luce, TERT. An. 17;
uestitus tota lege, Adu. Marc. 3, 15;
amictus lumine, VVLG. Ps. 103, 2;
induere (imperative) fortitudine tua, Is. 52, 1;
induere incorruptionem...immortalitatem, I Cor. 15, 53;

§23 **2.11** Singular collective or replacing a plural, very frequently or in a manner more surprising than in Classical Latin prose (cf. §7):

uniuersam uirginem compello, AVG. Serm. 191, 3, 'I speak to all the chaste young girls';

---

[10] It is by an analogous metonymy that certain terms come to indicate the action, e.g. *agnus ductus ad victimam*, HIER. Ier. 2, 11, 20, 'led to sacrifice' (σφαγή).

qui tollit peccatum mundi, VVLG. Io. 1, 29;
Christi lauat uestigium, AMBR. Ep. 41, 11, 'bathes the feet of Christ'.

§24 **2.12** Plural for the singular:
2.12.1 abstract words:
iudicariis seueritatibus, AMBR. Ep. 64, 84;
ariditates nostri pectoris, In Psal. 35, 22;
sibi licentias usurpant, AVG. Parm. 2, 3, 6;
2.12.2 concrete words:
liberasti plurimos de exsiliis, de carceribus, AMBR. Ep. 40, 25;
uiri sanguinum, VVLG. Ps. 5, 9 [? cp. Ps. 54, 24].

3 Etymological reaction[11]

§25 The meanings of certain words have been modified by a false etymological reaction, *mendum* 'lie' (Cl. Lat. 'error'), *dolus* 'pain' (Cl. Lat. 'trick'), *uiritim* 'by force' (Cl. Lat. 'by man'), *iterare* 'to travel' (Cl. Lat. 'to repeat'); *etc.*, confusions about which the dictionary will sufficiently inform us. But I should like to describe another kind of etymological reaction which is more a stylistic device of rhetoric: certain words suggest several meanings at once when the writer, giving to one term a particular new meaning, still has in mind at the same time the etymological meaning. For example, the word *statio* refers to the gathering together of Christians, the synaxis, and also to the fasting that accompanies the vigil of a holy day; but at the same time it is a gathering together where one remains standing, where one keeps watch while awaiting the Last Judgement or while repelling the attacks of the Devil, because the Church is also a camp:

die stationis...tubam angeli exspectemus orantes, TERT. Orat. 29;
castra nobis sunt nostra ieiunia, quae nos a diabolica infestatione defendunt: denique stationes uocantur quod stantes et commorantes in eis inimicos insidiantes repellamus, PS. - AMBR. Serm. 35.

Sacramentum 'oath, profession of faith, holy place, rite, faith, mystery, secret, sacred sign, sacrament', etc., is one of the terms of Christian Latin and Christian theology which has so many different meanings that are constantly implied, some implied in others, that it is very difficult to classify them. Christ, for Tertullian, is one 'person' *persona* of the Trinity, according to the traditional development of the language; but he is also the visible manifestation of the Father, the one through whom the Father speaks: *Ergo si Christus persona Paterni Spiritus est*, TERT. Prax. 14 (ed. Kr.). Here the writer has in mind the etymological meaning of *persona* 'the mask of the actor' through which he

[11] We are not concerned here with the etymological reaction of the type *assedens* for *assidens* and *reclaudo* for *recludo*.

speaks, and also the 'face' (figuratively). Analogous remarks could be made on the word *facies*.

The use of symbolic vocabulary, of which we shall say more later, leads likewise to these dualities of meaning. For Saint Augustine (*Trin. 12, 8, 13*), when Adam consents to eat the forbidden fruit, this is an abdication of the higher reason: *consentiente sibi capite suo, id est non eam* (*rationem* 'the lower reason') *cohibente atque refrenante illā* (the other 'higher reason', that kind of virility in the man) *quae in specula consilii praesidet quasi uirili portione.* It is then that he thinks of the expression of Saint Paul (*I Cor. 11, 3*): *caput autem mulieris, uir est.* In each couple, the man is 'the head'; in each man, 'the higher or virile reason' is 'the head'; the word *caput* simultaneously brings up two ideas, 'the seat of thought' and 'the seat of command', 'the head' and 'the authority' [*chef*]. A word has scarcely appeared under the pen when it begins to call up two or three different ideas; and, as the writer does not at all want to sacrifice any of this richness, the sentence becomes dense with meaning.

2 Traditional Rhetoric

§26 Since the traditional figures of rhetoric or of grammar were increasingly in favor at the end of the Empire, in secular writers as well as in Christian writers, their abundance will not reveal to us the originality of a new language or of a new style.

With regard to the figures of thought, I shall have occasion later to speak of metaphor, allegory, symbol, and the figurative style in general.

I have previously noted a certain number of metonymies or synecdoches (abstract for the concrete, singular for plural, etc.); the study of the syntax of subordinate clauses will give me the opportunity to point out certain parataxes.

It remains for me to give some examples of figures of speech and of grammar [*figures de mots et de grammaire*] that are found very frequently in Christian writers.

1. Hypallage or the substitution of words:

corniculatum lumen lunae, AVG. Ep. 55, 6 (= *corniculatae*); (the expression *inuisibiles oculi*, Tr. eu. Io. 74, 4, 'eyes which want to see only the invisible, eyes turned toward spiritual realities', is a kind of daring hypallage);

post noctem orationibus hymnisque *peruigilem*, OROS. Hist. 7, 36, 8;

a kind of popular hypallage:

diuitias absque *omnium* (in place of *omnibus*) iniquitatum generibus, TRACT. DE DIVIT. 17, 1 (Caspari, Briefe..., p. 53);

quem *alio* (in place of *alius*) generis argumento postea...occidit, VICT.-VIT. 1, 6, 21.

§27 **2.** Brachylogy, a shortened or abridged expression:

de uirgine exire, TERT. Virg. uel. 8, 'to cease to be virginal';

desinit uirginem, ibid. 11;

perorare uirum fortem, Val. 8, 'to perorate as a man of importance';

bestias lucrari, PASS. PERP. 14, 'to escape from beasts' (to die beforehand in prison);

alios non esse recipiendos praedicatores, quam Christus instituit, TERT. Praescr. 21, '... than those which' (absence of the article [pronoun-adjective *is*, cf. §131]);

Herodes...praefert supplicem, concogitat hostem, AVG. Serm. 152, 2 (Mai), 'he pretends to beg but thinks about war';

accelerare patrem, VICT. Aleth. 3, 556, 'to be impatient to be a father'.

§28 **3.** Anacoluthon:

istud quod...uoluptatum nugis animus occupatur uel plagis ac doloribus per corpus adfligitur, *adgrauari eandem et onerari* perspicuum est, MAMERT. St. an. 1, 22, 'when the soul is the prey of vain pleasures or when it is tormented by physical suffering, it is clear that it is weighed down and crushed' (in place of *adgrauare eandem et onerare*, the subject of which would be a *quod* clause);

et quicumque ex eius genere *homo...deficiunt oculi* eius..., AVG. Ciu. 17, 5.

§29 **4.** Prolepsis, in imitation of the Greek:

fecisti eas, ut ambularent, HIER. Tr. (Morin III, 2, p. 33);
animaduertite scripturam, quid significat, ibid. p. 68;
satanas expetiuit uos ut cribraret, VVLG. Luc. 22, 31;
Deus te scit quis sis, VIT. PATR. 5, 15, 66.

§30 **5.** Redundancy:

gratulari et gaudere, TERT. Pat. 11;
uani et superuacui, ibid. 8;
absolutio est et separatio, AMBR. Bon. mort. 8, 33;
ad...medelam sanationemque, HILAR. Psal. 134, 1;

or pleonasm:

addendo etiam insuper, AVG. Parm. 1, 11, 18;
ante praestruxerant, Bapt. 7, 2, 3;
dum sibi ipse origo nascendi est, HILAR. Trin. 9, 7.

§31 **6.** Different figures of repetition, anadiplosis, and recurrence [*reprise*]:

ut eum in Aegyptum transferat: Aegyptum idolis plenam, HILAR. Mat. 1, 6;

epanalepsis or recurrence at the beginning of each member:

nobis pater rogatur, nobis pater loquitur, Trin. 10, 71;

Anastrophe, when a word or a group of words is repeated at the beginning of the following member:

esse omnia in Deo, Deum in semetipso, Trin. 2, 31;

translation or polyptoton, when the word is repeated in a different case:

inopia pecuniae praestet...inopiam peccati, In Psal. 119, 8.

§32 **7.** More particularly, all the figures that form an antithesis will now present a certain originality because they have their point of departure in a 'new mentality'. The opposition of the body to the spirit appears earlier in the philosophy of Seneca; but in Christian Latin there appears the practice of opposing body to soul; flesh to spirit; spirit to matter; the life of this world, of these times, to the Christian life; earth to heaven; that which passes to that which lives eternally. This mentality is too well known to require many examples:

> quapropter noli, precor, irasci mihi, si te tantum diligo ut regnum, quod *temporaliter* assecutus es, uelim te habere *perpetuum*, et qui *imperas saeculo*, possis *regnare cum Christo*, GELAS. Ep. 12, 4 (to Emperor Anastasius).

Christian rhetoric, in general, enjoys indulging in parallel expressions and homeoteleuta:

> in pudicitia, flos *morum*, honor *corporum*, decor *sexuum*, TERT. Pud. in.;
>
> conseruantes firmiter Dominica mandata: in simplicitate *innocentiam*, in caritate *concordiam*, CYPR. Ep. 76, 2;
>
> eo nascenti superi nouo honore *claruerunt*, quo moriente inferi nouo timore *tremuerunt*, AVG. Serm. 199, 2.

The prayers of the liturgy in particular use antitheses and balanced periods with a certain majesty which, if one also takes into account metrical and rhythmical clauses,[12] bestows on these prayers the unmistakable charm of ceremonial Latin, all while residing in relatively simple language.

---

[12] Cicero, who had introduced oratorical rhythms to Rome, attached great importance to harmonious cadences and--especially at the ends of periods--to the metrical clausulae, which were later called the *cursus*. This practice was carried on after Cicero, and so also in the Christian writers, in St. Cyprian first of all. Others, like St. Augustine and St. Jerome, follow the rules for cadence with more or less regularity, according to the nature of their works. At approximately the time of St. Leon the *cursus* begins to follow stricter rules and to follow as formulaic models (e.g. in the Sacramentaries) certain documents of the imperial and pontifical chancelleries.

On this subject one could consult the article of L. Laurand, in his *Supplément au manuel des études grecques et latines*, 'Pour mieux comprendre l'antiquité classique', p. 60 ff.; see also the works cited in our Bibliography under the following names: Bornecque, di Capua, Delaney, Jouge, Mann, and Nicolau.

Here we call to mind only an essential difference: in the Classical period the cursus obeyed metrical rules, and it was determined solely by the quantity of the syllables, for example, the clausula that Cicero prefers, a trochaic metron preceded by a cretic: fīlĭī | cōmprŏ | bāvĭt.

At the end of the Empire, on the other hand, it is the accent that is the most important, and the allowable cadences are reduced to four types:

(1) *cursus planus*: accent on the 2nd and 5th syllables (from the end of the word group), e.g. *clementer exaudi*, SACRA. LEON. p. 120, 26.

(2) *cursus tardus*: accent on the 3rd and 6th syllables, e.g. quo*rum suffragiis*, *ibid.* p. 93, 1.

(3) *cursus uelox*: accent on the 2nd and 7th syllables, e.g. Do*mine Deus* no*ster*, *ibid.* p. 57, 17.

(4) *cursus dispondaicus*: accent on the 2nd and 6th syllables, e.g. do*na sentiamus*, *ibid.* p. 93, 2.

ut cuius in terra gloriam praedicamus, precibus adiuuemur in caelis, SACRAM. GELAS. 2, 59 (Feast of St. Michael the Archangel);

Deus, qui hanc sacratissimam *noctem ueri luminis fecisti illustratione clarescere*, SACRAM. GREG. 5, c. 29C (prayer for the Christ-mas Vigil; the same expression is found in Ennodius and the Gelasian Sacramentary, applied to the Easter Vigil);

qui *mortem* nostram moriendo destruxit et *vitam* resurgendo repara-uit, SACRAM. GREG. c. 92B.

§33 Unfortunately, the Church Fathers have had a tendency to multiply too generously antitheses and comparisons of words, some even rather forced, those figures which the Greeks called oxymoron and paranomasia:

pie irascentibus, HILAR. Psal. 51, 3;

tacita...exspectatio Deo *clamor* est, In Psal. 141, 2;

(Ambrosii) eloquia...ministrabant *sobriam* uini *ebrietatem* populo tuo, AVG. Conf. 5, 13, 23; this commonplace seems traditional be-cause St. Ambrose himself wrote in a hymn (7, 24):

laeti bibamus sobriam ebrietatem spiritus;

ructauere sacras ieiuno gutture laudes ebria corda Deo, P.-NOL. Carm. 27, 105.

St. Augustine enjoys stimulating his reader's attention by using puns:

o munde immunde, Serm. 105, 8;

non putemus, sed potemus, Serm. 119, 1;

onerant, non honorant, Serm. 8, 5;

cf. non onerant nos, sed ornant, SALV. Gub. 7, 2, 11.

§34 New words are coined to make this parallelism:

attende Petram nostrum, non funambulum, sed ut ita dicam, *mariambulum*, AVG. Psal. 39, 9 (speaking of St. Peter who at Jesus's call walked on the water);

cf. dissecrare 'to desecrate' opposed to: consecrare, PELAG. I Jaffé p. 983 (speaking of an excommunicant who wants to be consecrated as a true bishop).

3 Symbolism

§35 Another method of exposition particularly in favor among the Church Fathers is the symbol, which is more than just a simple rhetorical device. Undoubtedly, the taste for allegory and the practice of searching everywhere for symbols has already established itself in secular literature by this time. But in Christian writers, the symbol has a new importance: it has an exegetical foundation (1) when it was a matter of showing according to the teaching of St. Paul in a particular event, in a particular personage of the Old Testament, a prefiguring of what is realized in the New, and (2) when it was a matter of explicating the parables found in the Gospel. Abuse and artificiality appear when a writer wants to see symbols everywhere and to give every last detail significance, when the smallest incident, the most ordinary person, indeed the lowest animal is thought to require a mystical interpretation.

§36 Here are a few examples of the abuse of symbols. In the parable of the wise virgins and the foolish virgins, there is the number five. Why are there five foolish virgins and five wise virgins? asks St. Caesarius of his listeners. Well? It is because we have five senses, and he constructs an entire explanation on that number.[13] The same preacher, in sermon 34 (ed. Morin, p. 627), explains the parable of the Good Samaritan, and this is his allegorical interpretation: the beaten traveler is Adam; he is unhappy and fallen; the Good Samaritan is Christ, who rescues him and redeems him. So far we are within reasonable limits. But unfortunately, once he gets going on this road there is no stopping the good bishop; the allegory would become too simple. And we learn that the outlaws who have robbed the man are devils; that the inn, *stabulum*, to which the beaten man is brought, is the Church; that the inkeeper, *stabularius*, is St. Paul. And what will our preacher make of the horse, *iumentum*, who, he thinks, ought also to play a role in this affair? Very simple, it will represent...the incarnation! In Origen, by whom the Gallic preacher was

---

[13] In the *Moralia in Iob* Gregory the Great will abandon himself to trying to give one or more allegorical interpretations to the different numbers and to explaining in detail what the possession of seven sons, three daughters, five hundred pairs of oxen, three thousand camels, etc. indicates.

perhaps inspired, directly or not, the game is almost as complicated: *Samaritem, Christum; uulnera uero, inoboedientiam; animal, corpus Domini, etc.* HIER. *Orig. Luc. hom.* 34, c. 316D.

Thus—and this is a more serious point—this allegorical intemperance, inherited from the Greek Fathers and especially from Origen, is not the perquisite of secondary or medieval writers. Some oddities of this sort, perhaps a little less glaring, would be found in certain passages of St. Augustine or St. Ambrose. Both have spoken nobly of the symbolism of the Ark prefiguring the Church, but the latter is less fortunate when he compares, in imitation of Philo, the Ark to the human body: he is absolutely determined to forget nothing and to review the parts down to the hole of the buttocks, which is assigned the job of evacuating filth (Noe 8, 24; cf. 6, 14).

To be fair, certain happy discoveries might delight the modern reader, for example, the donkey which carries Jesus symbolizes uncultivated human nature having become 'the mount of God': *tot animarum ferocitates uectio Dei factae sunt*, HILAR. Mat. 21, 1.

This refining of the symbol, or simply the fact that the writer is filled with Biblical material, can lead also to a kind of verbosity. The quotations follow from one another, not called up by logical necessity, but by the pure association of words. The religious literature of the Middle Ages swarms with examples of this type; it is one of its charactertistics. But, that tendency exists already in the patristic period. Here is St. Ambrose speaking to the newly baptized: their rebirth in grace is compared to new youth (*Sacram.* 4, 2, 7), and quite naturally this verse comes to his lips: *Renouarbitur sicut aquilae iuuentus tua* (*Ps.* 102, 5); but the word *aquila* arouses in its turn another recollection, which is here hardly in keeping with the context: *ubi enim corpus ibi et aquilae* (*Mat.* 24, 28). Ambrose has perhaps noticed this because in the parallel passage of *De mysteriis* (8, 43), the first quotation will no longer call up the second; according to Dom Botte,[14] this could be explained by the fact that *De mysteriis* is a 'composed' work whereas *De Sacramentis* was not intended for publication.

§37 A grammarian does not have to discuss the value of patristic symbolism in itself, yet in many cases he will allow himself to say that we are looking at not so much an illusory exegesis as a decadent rhetoric. It is then that one regrets the disappearance of classical taste, of moderation, of appropriateness, or simply of good sense. Shall we say that what distinguishes the style of Christian writers from the classical style is that the latter has a monopoly on good sense? That would be a singularly unfair judgement. Look at the artificiality, for example, in all of Latin poetry, in spite of the great moderation that from time to time is reheated and served to the reader! Look at the abuse in dealing with the commonplaces of mythology! And, on the other hand, look at the rhetorical restraint in the letters of St. Leon, to cite only that

---

[14] In his edition of *De Sacramentis* in the collection *Sources chrétiennes*, no. 25, p. 12ff.

one writer! The Roman pontiffs are known to have preserved for a long time, well after the dark time of the invasions, the majesty and dignity of Latin prose, joined to an evangelical simplicity. The oldest liturgical texts, in the Leon and Gelasian Sacramentaries, are thoroughly imbued with these qualities, reverence here prohibiting preciosity. Christian Rome could be said to have remained the capital of good sense, if one considers the excesses of certain African writers of all periods or the 'Gallic buskin'[15] of the last Latin poets of the Merovingian period.

§38 After this digression I do not want to leave the symbol before having shown how it has influenced the vocabulary of Christian writers. St. Augustine remarked, for example, that in Genesis our first parents after their fall were ashamed of their nakedness and wove garments of fig leaves. The word *fig* will call up for him the idea of sin. So Jesus had said to Nathaniel: 'When you were under the fig tree, I saw you' (*Io.* 1, 48). *'Cum esses sub arbore fici uidi te,' tanquam diceret: cum esses in umbra peccati, Serm.* 89, 5. And in another sermon (69, 4): *ipse quippe Dominus Jesus sub ficu uidit omne genus humanum.* This is then a word which becomes in his language a symbol. But the associations of ideas multiply the symbols. Elsewhere (*Trin.* 12, 8, 13), the foliage symbolizes not only what covers shame but also uselessness because with regard to the fruit, which are good works, the leaf is only vanity: *tanquam folia dulcium fructuum, sed sine ipsis fructibus, ita sine fructu boni operis bona verba contexunt, ut male uiuentes quasi bene loquendo contegant turpitudinem suam.*

In Christian Latin the symbols of Biblical origin increase: Babylon will designate the world, opposed to the city of God; one is also aware of the names for Christ: the Lamb, the Husband. Other symbols bring us nearer to the figurative style of which we shall speak next. It is said in the book of *Proverbs* (21, 20): 'The precious treasures, the oil, are in the house of the wise man.' For the Hebrews oil is a sign of riches; it is still a nutriment (*Deut.* 32, 13); they used it equally for bathing, for lighting, for the anointing of kings, priests, et al. In the parable of the wise virgins, it is a question of oil and of the fact that the later virgins have taken care to fill their lamps with it. For the Fathers, oil will then be a symbol, a word which can be appropriately understood in a spiritual sense; it will designate riches and fertility; but especially moral ideas: Christian love shown in good works, gentleness, joy, justice, etc.:

absque oleo bonorum operum, HIER. Ep. 125, 19;
oleum misericordiae, CAES.-AREL. Serm. p. 621;

---

[15] An expression employed for the first time by St. Jerome (*Ep.* 58, 10), who is trying to characterize the grandiloquence of St. Hilary of Poitiers. But it applies most justly to the writers of the following centuries, and not only to Gallic writers. If Ennodius and Sidonius Apollinarius are affected poets, what is there to say about writers as baroque as Aldhelm and Gildas Sapiens? Their works truly mark the end and not the beginning of Medieval Latin literature because Medieval Latin literature was to produce, if not from the Carolingian Renaissance at least from the 12th cent., a flowering of remarkable Latin work.

cf. unxit te Deus oleo exultationis, Ps. 44, 8, ap. AVG. Psal. 82, 2 (*oleo laetitiae*, VVLG.).

The word *hyssop* becomes a symbol of purification:

aspergamus et nos hyssopo...et mundabimur a peccatis, PS.-RVF. (I.-Aecl.) Psal. 50, 9.

4 Figurative language

§39 That which, after all, constitutes the true originality of Christian Latin is not its grammar but its stylistics, understood with the meaning used by linguists and philologists such as Bally, Vendryes, and Marouzeau: a study of the expressive and emotional characteristics of the language. What makes the Latin which now concerns us a language quite different from Classical Latin is that we feel it circulate as a new warmth. The need to express, in the language, spiritual realities, and the desire of making these same realities intelligible to the humblest people, while basing them on concrete realities, caused an extraordinary flowering of figurative expressions; the love of God and the love of mankind enkindled an equal development of emotional expressions. Those are the two principle characteristics of Christian Latin. By figurative language, I mean words taken in a figurative sense as well as comparisons, metaphors, and allegories. In effect, the figurative sense of a word began by being a metaphor that then intruded on ordinary usage. In the Gospels and the other books of the New Testament, the kingdom of God is compared to a building; the supporters, to the stones of that building, of which Christ himself is the cornerstone; the word *aedificatio* will then metaphorically refer to the building of the Church, the kingdom of God, and afterwards the building of the faith in its own conduct and in that of others; and finally, the metaphor being forgotten, *aedificatio* will take on the abstract meaning of 'reinforcement', 'good example', 'edification'.

Certain abstract words were created to translate new ideas and concepts that Classical Latin, because of its emphasis on the concrete, could not express. As I said earlier, a large number of monographs have carefully pointed out all the new words in *-tas, -tio, etc.*, introduced by such and such a Christian writer; but we have not laid much stress on that other process which consists in taking up a concrete word, or one referring to concrete realities, to use it in a figurative or spiritual sense.

Our dictionary will show that these new meanings are infinitely more numerous than neologisms properly so called. One finds them in writings that are distinctly theological as well as in writings intended for the common people. However, statistics tell us without a doubt that the figures, comparisons, metaphors, and allegorical symbols are more frequent in sermons and exegetical works. Their increase in the matter which now concerns us is less a technique of rhetoric than the manifestation of an ardent desire to communicate the truths and sentiments with which the writer overflows.

It is the writer's need to express himself, the need to stimulate the imagination and touch the heart, that causes the transpositions to appear and the images to flow out. The Christian writer addresses not only the literature and people who live by their intelligence, but he wants also to speak to the heart and to be understood by all people, by all his brothers. In order to be understood by all, it is necessary for him to rely on the concrete realities that everyone has in front of him—in nature, in the sea, in the mountains, in the flowers of the field, in the fruits of the earth—and to rely on the realities that everyone could see in the diverse human activities—in the trades and professions, in the navy, in the army, in the law, in commerce, and even in the activities of the circus and athletic competitions.

It would require a catalogue to list all the images that have served to make his readers feel the action of God on his creatures, the love of Christ, the ugliness of sin, the beauty of Christian virtues, the baseness of the flesh, the grandeur of human destiny, the glory of the martyr, the happiness of heaven, etc.

§40 We shall content ourselves with bringing together here, by way of example, a choice of figurative expressions or images concerning a specifically Christian concept, that of sin, of moral wrong (*delictum, peccatum, culpa, uitium, noxa*).

It is a maggot:

tinea animae, CYPR. Zel. 7 (while speaking of jealousy);

particularly a stain, filth:

ut mundemus nos ab inquinamento carnis et sanguinis, TERT. Marc. 5, 12, 'to purify ourselves from the stains of the flesh and blood';
ab inquinamento carnis et spiritus, VVLG. 2 Cor. 7, 1[16];
libidinis inquinamentum, HIER. Orig. Ez. 9, col. 962;
immunditia, 'impurity of the person, corruption', even beyond cases where it is a question of lewdness properly so called;
nostra immunditia ad penetrandum secretorum Dei munditiam non sit indigna, GREG.-M. Hom. eu. col. 1143D;
coinquinatio spiritus, AVG. Serm. 45, 8, 'moral stain';
colluuio, Peccat. orig. 41, 47;
sanctificatum corpus detestabili colluuione uiolare, CYPR. Ep. 55, 26;
omnia haec mala communicant hominem, VVLG. Marc. 7, 23,'debase the person, stain him':
cf. communicat, id est, commune, profanum, ἀκάθαρτον facit, AVG. Faust. 16, 31;

[16] We do not distinguish Vulgate quotations from those of other translations. The Latin of the Vulgate has flowed into the current of Christian Latin.

omni culparum abstergine liber, PRVD. Apoth. 937;
uitia et peccata carnalia et terreni corporis infesta labes, CYPR. Zel. 14;
a peccati labe mundati, AVG. Peccat. merit. 3, 9, 17;

mire:

in luto prauitatis, GREG.-M. Hom. Ez. col. 872 A;

foulness:

sordes, TERT. Scorp. 12;
qui in sordibus est, VVLG. Apoc. 22, 11;
cf. sordesco, CASSIAN. Coll. 14, 16, 5; HILAR. Mat. 24, 7;
uitiis sordidamur, HIER. Ep. 75, 2;
uitiorum sordibus squalescere, PS.-AVG. Serm. app. 120, 1;

a flaw:

naeuus peccati, TERT. Carn. Chr. 16;

which it is necessary to wipe away, to efface, of which it is necessary to cleanse one's self, to purify one's self, to exculpate one's self:

abstergere, HIER. Ep. 61, 4;
se abstergere de immunditia peccatorum, PS.-HIER. M. 30, col. 586 C;
abluere, VVLG. Act. 22, 16; TERT. Paen. 6; AVG. Ciu. 1, 27;

ordinarily while speaking of baptism which is a *lauacrum*:

mundare, TERT. Pud. 2; AVG. Ep. 82, 18;
emundare, VVLG. Hebr. 9, 14; Io. 1 Ep. 1, 7; HILAR. Mat. 7, 2;
dealbare: si fuerint peccat uestra coccinum, quasi nix dealbabuntur, VVLG. Is. 1, 18; Ps. 50, 9;

which it is necessary to purify as by fire:

sordibus tuis tanquam igne decoctis, CYPR. Op. et el. 14.

Sin is also compared to a foreskin, by allusion to the spiritual circumcision of which St. Paul often speaks (e.g. Rom. 3, 29):

circumcidite praeputium cordis uestri, LACT. Inst. 4, 17, 18;

to a poison:

toxicum zeli, FVLG. ed. Helm p. 136, 12, 'the poison of jealousy';

to a strong drink that one consumes without batting an eyelid:

bibere iniquitatem, VVLG. Iob 1, 16;

to leaven:

expurgate uetus fermentum, VVLG. 1 Cor. 5, 7;

to a sickness:

omni sanato languore concupiscentiae carnis, AVG. C. du. ep. Pelag. 1, 11, 23;
lepra peccati, CAES.-AREL. Serm. Mor. p. 273, 25;
ut nisi renascendo liberari ab illa peste non possit, AVG. Nupt. et conc. 2, 38, 58;

to be able to free one's self from that plague only by the baptismal regenera-tion, while speaking of original sin (the word *pestis* in other respects more often means 'heresy'):

quos peccatorum similium pestilentia non corrumpit, AVG. Parm. 3, 2, 14;
tabes carnalis concupiscentiae, Peccat. merit. 1, 9, 10;
ab omni scelerum contagione semoti, ARN. 7, 48;
pectus purum ab omni contagione praestare, LACT. Inst. 6, 23, 16;

the same expressions with regard to original sin:

CYPR. Hab. uirg. 2; AVG. Peccat. merit. 3, 10, 18.

This sickness can be contracted:

sordes quascumque contrahimus eleemosynis abluamus, CYPR. Op et el. 1;
contrahere peccata, AVG. Parm. 2, 10, 20;
adtrahere, Nupt. et conc. 2, 4; Peccat. merit. 3, 9, 19.

By a kind of surgical operation, it is necessary to get rid of them, to amputate them:

radicitus amputare uitia, BEN. Reg. 33;
amputare passiones, AMBR. Noe 15, 55;
amputa opprobrium meum, VVLG. Ps. 118, 39;
amputatio macularum, TERT. Pud. 15;
amputatrix uitiorum, AMBR. Iob et Dau. 4, 3, 2.

Sin is insanity:

mentis alienatione dementes praecepta Domini contemnunt, CYPR. Laps. 33;

blindness:

discussa est omnis carnalium caecitas passionum, AMBR. Cain et Ab. 24, 16;

which causes us to fall:

clausis oculis impingere in odium, TERT. Apol. 3;
cf. lapis, impingat in quem uanitas, PRVD. Apoth. 45,

the obstacle against which vanity is going to stumble:

in alteram feminam impegit, TERT. Praescr. 30, 'fell for another woman, fell to this new passion';
fuerunt domini Israel in offendiculum iniquitatis, HIER. Ez. 13, 44, 9, they were a cause of scandal:
qui offendiculum tentationis intulerit, HILAR. Trin. 5, 9, 'who brought the scandal'.

The words *scandulum, scandalizare* are much more frequent in this sense.

Sin is an 'error' which leads us astray, out of the right path:

per itinera erroris, CYPR. Eccl. unit. 23; cf. TERT. Nat. 1, 16; PRVD. Cath. 6, 118;

sometimes through ignorance:

TERT. Paen. 2;
cf. a praestantiore conditore auersio, ad condita inferiora conuersio, AVG. Qu. ad Simpl. 1, 2, 18, the action of turning away from the Creator on high to creatures below.

Sin causes us to limp:

claudicauerunt a semitis suis, VVLG. Ps. 17, 46.

It is a fall:

casus, AVG. Psal. 129, 1;
qui post casum resurgunt, PACIAN. Ep. 3, 8;
multi enim cadere uolunt cum Dauid et nolunt surgere cum Dauid, AVG. Psal. 50, 3;
sine gratia cadit homo, Grat. 6, 13;
excidisse a mandato Dei, AMBR. Ep. 64, 14;

and, absolutely:

excidere, TERT. Paen. 6, fall into sin;
lapsus, AMBR. Obit. Th. 30;
lapsus linguae, VVLG. Eccli. 20, 20 and AVG. Perf. iust. 20, 43, 'sin in speaking'.

The word designates especially the sin of *lapsi*, of 'apostates':

CYPR. Laps. tit.; Ep. 56, 1: AVG. Ep. 78, 8;
labi a regula, TERT. Praescr. 3;

and absolutely:

labi hominis est, PRVD. Ham. 665;
lapsus in feminam, TERT. Praescr. 30;
in mulierem carne lapsus, Carn. Chr. 6, 'fallen into the sin of the flesh with a woman';
cadere in ruinam flagitiorum, AVG. Nupt. et. conc. 1, 16, 18;
ruinas animae sicut carnis reficere, An. et or. 4, 19, 29;
ne in damnabilia flagitia, id est in fornicationes uel adulteria conruantur, Nupt. et conc. 1, 14, 16;

a bond, a snare, a chain:

laquei peccati, Nupt. et con. 2, 13, 27;
a nexu peccati originalis absolui, An. et or. 1, 11, 14;
a contagione mortis antiquae et obligatione peccati, Ep. 190, 5; 157, 22;
in obligatione iniquitatis, VVLG. Act. 8, 23;
cf. adligare, ibid.;
delictis grauibus inuolutus, CYPR. Ep. 67, 5;
tantis iniquitatibus inuoluti, AVG. Parm. 3, 2, 10,

prisoners of very grave iniquities:

fascis pecccatorum, HIER. Ep. 60, 14;
nunquam praeuaricationis suae nos criniculis implicasset, AMBR. Parad. 2, 11, 'never would Eve have twisted us in the skein of her sin';

a pit:

incidunt in tentationem et muscipulam, CYPR. Orat. 14; COMM. Instr. 2, 7, 13;

a yoke, slavery:

quam misera seruitus seruire peccatis, AMBR. Nabuth. 6, 28;

especially while speaking of original sin:

uenundatus sub peccato, VVLG. Rom. 7, 14;
per originem primi hominis uenundati sub peccato, AVG. Peccat. merit. 1, 23, 33;

a debt:

absolutio debiti, GREG.-M. Dial. 4, 62;

that the Church can forgive, pardon:

dimissio delictorum, AVG. C. Iul. op. imp. 2, 15;
dimissio peccatorum, HIER. Ephes. 3, 5, 1;
dimittere peccata, VVLG. Luc. 11, 4;
dimittere delicta, TERT. Pud. 2.

The most common expressions are: *absoluere, soluere, absolutio.* Or indeed the sins can be restrained, bound:

alligare, VVLG. Mat. 18, 18;
potestas soluendi et alligandi, TERT. Pud. 21.

Another metaphorical meaning borrowed from the law: sin is an embezzlement, a betrayal, a violation:

praeuaricatio, HIER. Is. 1, 1, 2; etc.

This word is used also to refer to original sin:

praeuaricatio mandati; FILASTR. 116; HIER. Ep. 121, 8.

It is necessary to bridle sins, to buckle them in:

supremam carni fibulam imponere, TERT. Monog. 3, 'impose the supreme restraint on the flesh';
uoluntariis delictis laxare fibulam, Cor. 11, 'loosen the bridle on intentional errors';

to engage in a struggle with them:

congressio cum uitiis, AVG. C. Iul. 2, 8, 23;
mens congressionis ignara, ENNOD. Ep. 3, 21;
spiritalibus nequitiis congredi, CASSIAN. Inst. 5, 16, 1,

to struggle against the spirits of evil. But the words *congressio* and *congredi* are applied more often to the constant struggle by the martyrs.

Sin is a fire, a fever:

feruura peccati, TERT. Scorp. 5;

a boiling:

ebullire in omnem libidinem, TERT. Marc. 1, 37, 'heat up from all the passions';

it is necessary to calm this fever:

nisi prius ignis concupiscentiae a mente deferueat, GREG.-M. Ep., ed. Ewald II, p. 340, 24.

Inversely, sin is compared to cold:

frigus, HIER. Mat. 25, 7;
qui peccati frigore mortuus est, BACHIAR. Repar. laps. 7;
cf. infidelitatis frigus, MAMERT. St. an. 2, 7;

to a hardening:

quibus teneritas conscientiae obduratur in callositatem uoluntarii erroris, TERT. Nat. 2, 1, 'by which the delicacy of conscience hardens into the callousness of voluntary error';
obdurato corde, CASSIAN. Coll. 9, 30, 1;

to a numbness:
duritia cordis obdormitio est, AVG. Psal. 75, 10;

to poverty:
mendicitas, Ord. 1, 2, 3;

to an arid desert:
de ariditate peccati ad loca pascuae perductus, CASS. Psal. col. 167B, 'leads from the desert of sin to the abodes of plenty';

to anarchic outgrowth:
unde talia uitia siluescerent, AVG. Ciu. 2, 18, 3;
siluescere ausus sum uariis et umbrosis amoribus, Conf. 2, 1, 1;

that it is necessary to make it dry up on the spot:
uoluptatem carnis arefacere, GREG.-M. Hom. Ez. col. 955C;

to a cutting from a plant, *tradux*, while speaking of the transmission of original sin,
AVG. Peccat. merit. 2, 2, 2;

to a tare sown in the heart:
auena, HIER. Ep. 130, 7;

to bitterness:
carnalis concupiscentiae ipsas eius amaritudines amamus, GREG.-M. Hom. eu. 28, 3, 'to love even the bitterness of carnal concupiscence';

to rust:
aegra pectoris robigo, PRVD. Cath. 7, 205;
cf. aeruginat nequitia illius, VVLG. Eccli. 12, 10,

its malice is like rust (which constantly comes back).

Sin causes one to resemble a beast:
statim ut mulieres uiderint, hinniunt, HIER. Iou. 50;
post transeuntes feminas...adhinnire, AVG. Mor. Manich. col. 1374.

It is a Biblical metaphor:
Ier. 5, 8;
cf. ascendit corporis uoluptates, AMBR. Hel. 5, 10, 'it mounts carnal pleasures';
caninae nuptiae, HIER. Ep. 69, 2, 'shameful sexual relations'.

Sin is itself a devouring beast:
sin autem uitia nos quasi quaedam bestiae fuerint depraedatae, HIER. Is. 1, 1, 8, 'but if we let ourselves be devoured by our vices as by savage beasts';

as the sinner:
peccata uidelicet leuia uitantium et grauia deuorantium, HILAR. Mat. 24, 7, 'the sins of those who avoid slight faults but swallow serious ones without remorse'.

It is a weight that burdens us:

ne praeponderent uos peccata uestra, VVLG. 4 Esdr. 16, 77;

carnis onere praegrauatus, AVG. Serm. 6, 1 (Mai), 'worn out under the weight of the flesh';

a coarseness, a moral awkwardness:

humanae mentis crassitudine hebetatum, ENNOD. Hart. p. 380.

Those who conceive it are made pregnant by it, impregnated:

praegnans est qui res alienas concupiscit, CAES.-AREL. Serm., Mor. p. 594, 8;

cf. impraegnari, ibid. p. 594, 17, 'conceive an evil thought'.

Sin is a place of exile far from God:

exsulare Deo, AMBR. Ep. 64, 100;

an abyss:

abyssus, AVG. Conf. 1, 1, 1;

an evil invention, a perverse trick:

adinuentiones, HIER. Ephes. 3, 6, 11;

ideo fructum adinuentionum uestrarum comedetis, In Is. 2, 3, 1;

cf. VVLG. Iud. 2, 10; AVG. Ciu. 17, 4;

a goad, while speaking of envy:

stimulus inuidiae, AVG. Spir. et litt. 2, 3.

It is, moreover, the envy of death:

stimulus mortis peccatum, VVLG. 1 Cor. 15, 55 (cf. Rom. 5, 12).

It is itself death:

quid te in lapsum mortis cum serpente quem colis sternis? CYPR. Ad Demetr. 16, 'why let yourself sink into the mortal fall with the serpent you adore?';

mori, AVG. Parm. 2, 10, 22;

opera mortis, TERT. Pud. 2;

exspirare in haeresim, Pud. 19, 'to throw one's self into the death of heresy';

animam tuam perdidisti...et ipsa ambulans funus tuum portare coepisti, CYPR. Laps. 30, '...and while walking, you began to carry your corpse';

cum multo profundius etiam mendacio simulationis absumptus sit, AVG. C. Cresc. 2, 26, 31, 'when his spiritual death is still more profound, if he hides it with a lie'.

Finally, it is necessary to die to sin:

mori peccato, VVLG. Rom. 6, 2;

moriuntur homines culpae ueteri et iniquorum operibus, AMBR. Ep. 50, 10;

mors criminum, CYPR. Ad Don. 4;

caro concupiscentiis moritur, LEO-M. Serm. 13;

to crucifiy it:

carnalia crucifigere, PS.-CYPR. Sing. 40;

crucifixerunt corpus cum uitiis et concupiscentiis, HILAR. Mat. 10, 25.

The accumulation of these various examples, separated from their context, produces necessarily an impression of incongruity, the more so as certain writers enjoy heaping up images with little self-control; here is how one preacher denounces jealousy: *inuidia malum uetustum, prima labes, antiquum uirus, saeculorum uenenum, causa funeris*, PETR.-CHRYS. *Serm. 4, c. 194 B.*[17]

Moreover, one could have pointed out more poetic images while singling out 'the Christian virtues' or 'the martyr'. An entire book would be necessary if one wished to review all the figures which attempt to translate Christian thought and feeling about God, Christ, people like St. John the Baptist, St. John the Evangelist, St. Paul, about the human body, the intimacy of the conscience, death, heaven, about the world, the Devil, etc. This astonishing profusion—hardly up to the standards of classical taste which requires more moderation in prose—is most often not due to the desire to be conspicuous, but much more to the desire to convince and to edify, and so due to a great need of expressing ideas and feelings.

---

[17] The same writer declares, while speaking of the fast (*Serm.* 8, c. 209): *est ieiunium castitatis murus, pudicitiae propugnaculum ciuitas sanctitatis*... and he thus displays his virtuosity in a good ten lines. Later, the book of *Synonyms* of Isidore of Seville will be entirely composed of this sort of accumulation, but it is, without a doubt, a scholarly work.

5 Emotional Language

§41 Let us move on to the other essential aspect of Christian Latin, the development in the old vocabulary of numerous new emotional meanings parallel to the creation of certain neologisms intended to convey the feeling of 'Christian love' [*charité*].

Obviously, affection, tenderness, and love are feelings too natural, too human, not to be in full bloom in certain secular works before Christianity. There is a Vergilian sweetness. The deceased young woman of Propertius (IV, 12ff.), who speaks from the depths of the tomb to the small infants that she has left on the earth to urge them to be affectionate towards their father even if he remarries, to comfort his old age if he remains widowed—that deceased young woman expresses herself with a forgetfulness of self, with the tenderness of an exquisite soul—I was going to say Christian soul.

But one can, nevertheless, say with certainty that this sensibility acquired, in the language of Christians, a new warmth and that it appears so consistently in all periods that it leaves its own particular imprint, its own special tonality. We shall try to characterize this sensibility without moving beyond the domain of linguistics into that of literature.

Emotional language appears in syntactic turns, in the position of words, in exclamations, interjections, and particles; but since these stylistic devices, although frequent in Christian writers, are not peculiar to them, I prefer to draw attention to a selection of words to which Christianity has given a new emotion or which it has created to express new feelings.

Here the influence of the text of the Bible, i.e. the first or later translations of the Vulgate, has been a determining factor because it contains already all of the essence of the Christian tonality. The emotional character of the style of the Bible was keenly felt by Augustine, who sets it against the intellectual style of secular philosophers: *non habent illae paginae (Platonis) uultum pietatis huius, lacrymas confessionis...(Conf.* 7, 21, 22). If the Old Testament is compared to Greek and Latin secular literature, the first difference which strikes us, especially in the Psalms and the prophetical works, is a passionate feeling of attachment to God, an ardent appeal to him, an enthusiastic confidence in his protection. In the New Testament, in addition to Christian love [*charité*], the love of mankind and the attachment to Christ are also expressed.

1 Mystical love

§42 It is necessary to say, first of all, that in Christian Latin, the prayers of the liturgy, the meditations, the hymns, and particularly the moving supplications in the Middle Ages inspired by the devotion to the Virgin Mary—all of that constitutes a language totally different, because of its emotional qualities, from secular Latin. But since liturgical Latin developed further in a later period of the Middle Ages, I am obliged to restrict myself to some examples taken from the patristic period.

All languages in the advanced phase of their development have a tendency to increase the number of words compounded with a preposition. This expressive impulse here fits well with the desire to set forth the mystic fervor. The preposition *ad* indicates already by itself one direction; it seems to translate an emotional movement towards God, in expressions like:

totus ad Deus eram,[18] HIER. Tr. I in psal. p. 157, 6;
ingemiscere ad Deum, SALV. Gub. 7, 11;
fiduciam habemus ad Deum,[19] VVLG. Io. 1 Ep. 3, 21 (πρὸς τὸν Θεόν).

And in composition:

*ac*corporari in Christo, P.-NOL. Ep. 4, 1;
quis mihi dabit *ad*quiescere in te? AVG. Conf. 1, 5, 5.

The context gives to this compound verb an emotional force that is more pronounced than in this example:

non adquiescit sanis sermonibus Domini, 1 Tim. 6, 3, 'he does not have trust in...'
adhaerere Deo is a Biblical expression that St. Augustine brings up and comments on again and again (see the dictionary for the words adhaereo, adhaesio, inhaereo).

The preposition *cum*, in composition, expresses in certain cases a reconciliation of the divinity towards us or our desire to unite with it, to share, for example, the sufferings of Christ:

commortuus est Domino suo, HIER. Ep. 22, 39;
qui Christo commoritur, AMBR. Apol. Dau. II, 3, 7.

In the dictionary other examples can be found of words like *compatior* and *complaceo*. A certain number of new terms have been compounded with this preposition: *complacatio, condelectatio, condescensio, conglorifico, conglorior, consepelio, consurgo,* and *conuiuifico*.

Compound adjectives, such as *indeficiens, indeflexibilis, indesinens, ineffabilis, incommutabilis,* and *immarcescibilis*—and all the compounds with a

---

[18] Cf. with the preposition *in*, and note the emotional force of the repetition of *totus*:
in Deum uiribus totis ac toto corde suspensus, CYPR. *Ad Don.* 5.

[19] In expressions like *oratio ad Patrem, credere ad*, one will find not so much an emotional tendency as a grammatical use analogous to *dicere ad, loqui ad, etc.*

privative *in-*, often modeled on the Greek, designating the attributes of God—translate the enthusiasm for what does not come to an end, the need of the absolute.

Analogous remarks could be made about the compounds in *prae-* and in *super-*. Undoubtedly, with regard to what concerns the divinity, some of these compounds have been created to express theological concepts such as *prae-exsistentia, praedestinatio, praeprincipium, supercoelestis, supernaturalis* (of the 6th cent.), *etc.*; but others have a purely emotional force, such as *praeclareo, praeconspicabilis, superabundantia* (of grace), *superlaudabilis et supergloriosus in saecula (Dan. 3, 53).*

Certain new words compounded with *bene-* express the acceptance of the will of God, of what he has determined, while emphasizing the fact that all that he wills is good: *beneplacens, beneplacitum,* and *benesentio.*

With the exception of some compounds, few new words were created in the domain of the mystic sensibility, and most come from Greek, such as *ecstasis* (at least in one of the senses), *clerus, eucharistia,* and *euangelium.* These last three seem to be from pure Ecclesiastical Latin, but in reality they possessed, from their origin, an emotional force which was felt in the first centuries:

> clerus 'the clergy', but etymologically (κλῆρος) the legacy of the Lord;
> eucharistia 'eucharist', but etymologically (εὐκαριστία) action of grace, a meaning which appears in Tertullian and St. Jerome;
> euangelium 'gospel', but etymologically (εὐαγγέλιον) good news, a meaning found up to the ninth century;
> Gabrihel mundi gaudii optulit euangelium, ANAST.-BIBL. Chron. (ed. Boor p. 61);

moreover, when a person read *praedicare euangelium,* he did not understand it with the cold meaning of 'preach the gospel', but much more: 'to proclaim everywhere and more loudly the good news of the kingdom of God'; there is an echo of the lyricism of St. Paul writing *beati pedes euangelizantium pacem!*

More numerous are Classical Latin words which, by themselves or taken in context, release a new warmth. Examples of this new warmth can be found in the words *affectus, benignitas, caritas, confiteor, credo, desiderator, desideratus, dilectio, dilectus, dilecta, Dominus, inuidia, miseratio, misericordia, prouidentia* (although God the provider—in the Christian sense of *provident*—may be more often called to mind by words like *largitior* and *dispensator*), *timor, uisito, etc.* Thus the word *Dominus*, in speaking of Christ, will no longer express the harshness of a master; it is usually joined to epithets like *misericors* and *miserator* or simply *pius, dulcis*, and *bonus. Misericordia* means 'pity, mercifulness' in Cicero as well as in our writers, but the stylistic force is entirely different if God, for example, is called *fons omnium misericordiarum* (AVG. *Psal.* 6, 10); the intensive plural has a Biblical quality: *mirifica misericordias tuas*, VVLG. Ps. 16, 7. The emotional force of this term is still more heightened when it is read in association with other words, that is, synonyms or words with an analogous meaning. We have talked about redundancy, but this is not a gratuitous redundancy: *misericordias tuas et clementiam tuam*, RVF. Greg. orat. p. 250, 7; *pietas misericordiae*, LEO-M. Serm. 55, 5; or *miseratio clementiae*, Serm. 12, 2. The frequent repetition of these emotional expressions plays a part in giving the Christian style its proper tonality.

Finally, figurative language translates in its turn passionate mystical aspirations:

amplector 'to become devoted to': a. Christum, CYPR. Mort. 3;
dilectione amplectere (imperative) Deum, AVG. Trin. 8, 8, 12;
ut unum bonum meum amplector te, Conf. 1, 5, 5;
anhelo 'to yearn towards': anhelant (literae tuae) sitim tuam et desiderium...animae tuae in atria Domini, P.-NOL. Ep. 44, 2;
cf. tibi (Deo) suspiro die ac nocte, AVG. Conf. 7, 10, 16;
clamo 'to cry, to call upon with great cries, to supplicate';
deficio 'to lose strength';
esurio 'to be hungry for';
flammesco 'to blaze up';
immolo 'to immolate' (in speaking about spiritual offering, such as penitence and prayer);
inebrio 'to intoxicate';
glutinor 'to become attached to';
inuiscero 'to implant deeply in the heart'.

The desire for heaven is expressed in images which express the nostalgia of those who are on earth, of exiles *exsules*, of colonists *coloni* (see also *incolatus*), of travelers *uiatores* (see also *peregrinatio, peregrinor*), far from their fatherland *patria, politeuma*; heaven is a place of rest *repausatio, requies*, a coolness *refrigerium*, peace *pax*; glory *gloria, palma*, in the mansion of God *domus, mansio, aula, tabernacula aeterna*, where we will see God face to face *facie ad faciem*, without a mirror, without puzzlement *sine speculo, sine aenigmate*. Death no longer seems to be a dreadful thing: it is simply a departure *migratio* (*migrare, recedere*), a passage *transitio* (*transire*), a sleep *dormitio* (*dormire*), or a recalling to God *accitus, uocatio* (*uocare*).

The Christian language has tried hard to feel God, not a remote God or an object of discussion for the intellect of philosophers, but a God close to the soul. We are fully aware of the figurative and allegorical expressions referring to the humanity of Christ, such as *agnus* and *pastor*. St. John's act of leaning on the breast of the Master has powerfully affected imaginations and hearts; in one inscription, he is called *accubitor Dei*, (ROSSI II, p. 258);

cf. cubator Dominici corporis, P.-NOL. Carm. 21, 4;
in Domino Iesu, exemplo Ioannis, ut haec possimus sentire et colloqui, accubemus, HILAR. Trin. 2, 21.

To express the benevolence of God, some almost familiar acts are sketched out in the imagination of the writer, who has been influenced by the Biblical style:

Deus abstergit uulnera humana, PETR.-CHRYS. Serm. 36, c. 301 (absterget Deus omnem lacrymam, Apoc. 7, 17; cf. Is. 25, 8).

He stoops to receive the martyr, his guest:

cum sit Dominus susceptor animae meae, AVG. Serm. 334, 1.

He knocks at the door of our heart:

pulsator aurium mearum, Conf. 10, 31, 46;

cf. animam semper Deus alloquitur, animam compellit atque aduocat ut animum sibi aduertat, TERT. An. 13.

And while speaking of the Bible:

sic loquitur ut...ueritate magnos pascat, affabilitate paruulos nutriat, AVG. Gen. litt. 5, 3.

Teneritas pietatis Dei, SALV. Gub. 8, 3, 17,

alludes to the tenderness of God who watches over his creatures 'as the apple of his eye':

(custodi me ut pupillam oculi, Ps. 16, 8; cf. Zach. 2, 8).

In the dream of Saturus, the Good Shepherd, a venerable old man seated on his throne, receives the martyrs; these draw near, they embrace him; and he, in turn, leans toward them to caress their faces with his hand:

et osculati sumus illum et de manu sua traiecit nobis in faciem, PASS. PERP. 11.

2 The love of mankind, human love

§43 Here also compounds with the prefix *cum* are much in favor, either to reinforce the meaning of the simple word or to signify in a more expressive way the union with our brothers, with their joys and their sufferings, e.g. *coadiuuo, concateno, conexio*; as well as some new words: *coaegroto, coanhelo, coexsulto, coinfirmor, collaetor, commartyr, commembrum, commeus, compau-per, complacentia, condescensio, congaudeo.*

The dictionary will indicate the new terms, such as *eleemosyna, refocillo, refrigerium*; and also the old terms which have taken on a new emotional meaning, such as *affectio, affectus, filiolus, frater, fraternitas, fraternus, germanus, glutinum, infans, mansuetudo, merces, misericordia, osculum, pacificus, parturio, sollicitudo, unanimitas, unio, uiscere, etc.*

Some examples will allow us to see the manner of this evolution: *caritas*[20] earlier, in classical Latin, means 'affection, love'; but the way in which this term is now combined with others or inserted into a figure gives it an entirely different stylistic force:

plenam et paternam dulcedinem caritatis, CYPR. Op. et el. 18 (dulcedo has taken on the meaning of 'love, affection': suorum paruulorum dulcedo, Ad Fort. 7);

amor fraternus et caritas, RVF. Clem. 8;

parturiens paruulos mater caritas, AVG. Tr. ep. Io. 2, 4;

fraternae inuicem caritatis, HILAR. Mat. 8, 80.

---

[20] See in particular the thesis of Mlle. Pétré, *Caritas*, mentioned in our Bibliography.

The word *dilectio*, which in like manner translates ἀγάπη, could give rise to analogous remarks:

frigus odiorum dilectionis calore mutare, HIER. Ep. 98, 28;
ad nostram inter nos dilectionem, P.-NOL. Ep. 11, 5;
pacem et dilectionem sectantes, NICET. Spir. 22.

Fraternus is associated frequently with those two terms as well as *pax*, *concordia*, and *amor*:

caritas fraterna, CYPR. Eccl. un. 14;
dilectio fraterna, Ep. 59, 1;
fraternus amor et caritas, RVF. Clem. 8.

In the following formula, it is the metaphor which warms the expression:

sit pax dilecta uestra et amica, AVG. Serm. 357, 1.

Benignus is quite classical, but the group of words *benigno corde* (CAES.-AREL. *Serm. Mor.* p. 163, 27) is no longer classical.

The epithets *carus* and *dilectus* demand that they be used in the superlative to satisfy fully the emotional intention; afterwards the use became stereotypical in homilies. Already in the work of Pliny the Younger, *inuicem* could express the reciprocity of emotion; it became a very frequent use in Christian Latin with all sorts of verbs:

suscipite inuicem, VVLG. Rom. 15, 7;
inuicem uos ametis, HIER. Ep. 7, 1;
inuicem fratres mutua tolerantia foueant, CYPR. Bon. pat. 15;
crimina inuicem donare, AVG. C. Gaud. 1, 37, 47, 'to pardon mutually their wrongs'.

The human emotions are ennobled by the religious feeling if one associates the Lord with the feeling, in a formula like

dilectissimum meum in Domino, VVLG. Rom. 16, 8,

a formula often reproduced. Finally, the word *pax*, in some expressions of Biblical origin, gives to the formula of greeting a kind of religious serenity:

et osculatus est me et dixit mihi: filia, pax tecum, PASS. PERP. 10 (cf. et dicit eis: pax uobis, Luc. 24, 36).

Other words have slipped toward a distinctly new emotional meaning, and so *pietas* will designate not only the 'benevolence' of God towards mankind, but also the 'benevolence', the 'Christian love', and the 'beneficence' of human relations:

pietas abesse christiano qui potest? P.-NOL. Carm. 10, 85 (in speak-ing of the duty of emotion);
pietas proprie Dei cultus... more autem uulgi hoc nomen etiam in operibus misericordiae frequentatur, AVG. Ciu. 10, 1;
uiscera pietatis ignorauit (the rich evil person), GREG.-M. Hom. eu. 40, 3;

nevertheless he will understand distinctly only the meaning of 'pity' in Medieval Latin.

Sedulitas expresses not only 'willingness', 'zeal', but also 'friendly faithfulness', e.g. AMBR. Abr. 1, 5; 'amiability', 'courtesy', 'graciousness', e.g. MABR. Off. 1, 20; 1, 37; especially in this example:

angelus uenit ad Mariam et cum sedulitate et gratia uenit, Abrah. 2, 9.

Anima means 'soul, emotion, intimacy of the heart':

cur ergo me excruciat desiderium tui apud ipsam intus animam? AVG. Ep. 27, 1. Under the influence of Biblical expressions (e.g. anima Ionathae conglutinata est animae Dauid, I Reg. 18, 1), this word can become the equivalent—but more emotional—of the personal pronoun:

si quis beneficiat animae meae, FILASTR. 134, 2.

Even more new meanings in the epithets *beatus* and *benedictus*, when one speaks of the dead, especially while blessing the memory of martyrs:

fortissimi et beatissimi CYPR. Ep. 11;
beatae recordationis, CAELEST. I Ep. 21, 8;
sub episcopatu Eleutherii benedicti, TERT. Praescr. 30.

Moreover, *benedictus* is used also when one is addressing the living:

consideremus itaque, benedicti, TERT. Orat. 1 (Biblical formula: cf. Gen. 24, 31; Luc. 1, 42).

As to epistolary formulas, at the end of the Empire they had become much longer and more ceremonious than in the classical period, and so they took on a conventional appearance; nevertheless, one can say that they have often been influenced by the style of Christian love, where respect is obliged to unite with emotion:

dilecte fili;
carissime frater;
desiderantissimus or desiderandissimus;
carissimi in Christo fratres;
beatissime et uenerande papa;
deocolentissimo episcopo (θεοσεβής);
deoamicissimo uiro (θεοφιλής), etc.

The play in these expressions is extremely varied; students have devoted several dissertations to them. An abbess, in her account of her voyage to holy places, addresses her sisters in the course of the narration in this way:

dominae uenerabiles sorores, PEREG. 2, 8;
dominae, lumen meum, ibid. 23, 10 (mea lux is also from the pre-vious historical period).

Notice, finally, in conversation, these formulas:

fac, abba, charitatem, et dic mihi sermonem, VIT. PATR. 7, 2, 3, 'please be so kind as to tell me something...';
domina soror, PASS. PERP. 4, 'lady my sister' or 'my dear sister', these are expressions used by the brother of Perpetua;
curre, domne meus, VICT.-VIT. 2, 30, spoken by a grandmother to her grandson to cheer him up.

It seems then that the last appellation has taken on an affectionate tone. St. Augustine, in a sermon (14, 3, 4), speaks to a pauper in this way:

domne pauper 'dear pauper';

but he is thinking also of the 'eminent dignity of the poor man,' who represents Christ.

§44 Obviously this sweetness, and even in certain cases this graciousness, is not as widely seen as other styles; certain writings dealing with controversial topics, particularly in the work of Tertullian or Jerome, are rather caustic. Moreover, one cannot speak of a uniform Christian language. There is the language of inscriptions, which can be from Vulgar Latin or from erudite poetry; the language of the first acts of the martyrs; the language of the works of Tertullian, too peculiar for us to be able to say that he is the creator of Christian Latin; the language of the first translations of the Bible, and there is variety there also, if one refers to the different quotations which the Fathers have made from them and that information which different mansucripts have preserved for us; it is the first Christian Latin—essentially a language of translation—before the appearance of letters such as those of Tertullian, Lactantius, and Cyprian. Later one will be able to recognize the Latin of familiar homilies, the Latin of theological controversies, which takes great pains to translate Greek, liturgical Latin, which will preserve the essence of Christian Latin, and the official Latin of the pontifical chancellery. Each writer ultimately has his own proper language in so far as it is original; one can even say that St. Augustine has many: immediately after his conversion he remained relatively Ciceronian; the language of his theological writings is not that of his sermons, the latter being very simple and not avoiding vulgarisms such as *nunquam fecit tale frigus* (*Serm.* 25, 3). Likewise, the homilies that St. Jerome delivers before the monks of Bethlehem are in a freer Latin than that in his other writings.

§45 Yet certain texts like those of the Bible, the work of certain writers like St. Cyprian, St. Augustine, and St. Jerome—which were copied incessantly—have contributed to a kind of common Christian language which remains very much alive all the way to the end of the Middle Ages.[21] Now the

---

[21] This period certainly witnessed monstrous excrescences in the domain of vocabulary. In the Carolingian period new Greek words were introduced, either artificially by certain poets, with the help of lexicons, or more naturally in Italy, through relations with Constantinople: e.g. *adelphus, exas* and *exafoti*. In the thirteenth century St. Thomas Aquinas reinstated some Greek terms: e.g. *andragathia*. Some Arabic words, such as *amireus* and *amiras*, appeared in Anastasius Bibliothecarius and later in the period of the Crusades. But it is especially the chroniclers and more still the jurists who contribute to the corruption of the language by introducing, *en masse*, according to their nationality, German, English, French, Spanish, and Italian words more or less rigged out with Latin endings. No more annoyance with the Latin! If a writer does not know the word *messor*, he writes *falcator*; in lieu of *tumor*, he will in the same way take *enflura*. Scholastic philosophy, in its own way, created a very special vocabulary; if it appears to offer a certain technical perfection to the eyes of the specialist, it will all be repelling as literature. Nevertheless, let us not deceive ourselves. The

impression which emerges from this necessarily superficial overview, superficial if one considers the immensity of this literature created by writers so different and belonging to time periods so different—the impression that emerges is that these two characteristics, the development of a figurative language and the warming of emotional expressions seem to be the most constant: they are the characteristics which create an atmosphere of affinity between the very old writings, like the *Passio Perpetuae*, and those of the mystics of the Middle Ages, such as St. Bernard and St. Bonaventure, or of the hagiographers like Thomas de Celano, without mentioning lesser writers. One can object that I am nearing the end of this discussion and that the question of proving the originality of a Christian literature has not been brought up; but I think I have remained within the limits of this overview, because the domain of stylistics is still that of language. So, one can speak of a language of Christian writers, or more simply of Christian Latin, on the condition of specifying precisely, as we have just done, the idea behind this term. It is always Latin, and when Meillet (*Esquisse d'une histoire de la langue latine,* p. 280) declares, 'Between the very classical language and that of the Vulgate or of the Fathers of the Church, there are only differences of detail', he is right in the purely grammatical domain; on the other hand, in the domain of vocabulary and stylistics there are more than differences of detail. In this christened Latin we recognize the old classical language, but a language which, while carrying the stigma of a certain decadence, has been nevertheless rekindled in spite of everything and has acquired a new life; it is like that of a new people, this *populus christianus*, who, thanks to the language, have guarded for ten centuries the consciousness of their unity.

---

purely mystical writers wrote a language which would not have much puzzled a contemporary of St. Augustine.

Part Two: Grammatical Observations

Morphology[22]

1 Declension

§46 **1.1** Increased use of Greek declensions: in the first declension, the accusatives *phantasian, latrian, etc.*; the nominatives *tetrarches, cataractes;* in the second declension the neuters *charadrion, epinicion, topazion, etc.*; in the third, the numerous nouns in *-is*, gen. *-eos*, dat. *-ei*, acc. *-in*, gen. pl. *-eon*, such as *haeresis, exomologesis, decapolis, etc.*; and the numerous singular accusatives in *-a*, acc. plur. *-as*, as in classical poetry.

§47 There is no lack of doublets: *leuites* and *leuita*; *pascha, -ae* and *pascha, -atis*; *botrus, -i* and *botrys, -yos*; *cratera, -ae* and *crater, -eris*; *lampada* and *lampas, etc.*; with all the more reason in proper nouns:
Eleusis and *Eleusina.*

§48 **1.2** Some Hebrew plurals in the Vulgate: *Cherubim*, Gen. 3, 24, plur. of *Cherub*, Ex. 25, 19; *Philisthiim*, Gen. 10, 14, beside *Philisthaei*, 1 Par. 10, 2.

§49 **1.3** Increase of forms in *-abus* in the first declension: *animabus, asinabus.*

§50 **1.4** In the second declension, the vocative *meus* is found frequently, instead of *mi.*

§51 **1.5** In the third declension, genitives in *-um*, instead of *-ium*: *apum, prolum, pauentum, peccantum*;

---

[22] These are only the most general remarks, the details being the concern of the dictionary.

inversely, *plebium* for *plebum, etc.*

§52 **1.6** Neuter ablatives in *-e*, instead of *-i*, *dulce, conclaue*; and, inversely, of ablatives in *-i*, instead of *-e*, *in ueteri testamento*; especially in the comparatives: *inferiori, priori, etc.*

§53 **1.7** In the fourth declension, ablatives in *-ui*, instead of *-u* (less common), *sexui suo despoliari*, TERT. *Val.* 32;
and, inversely, some datives in *-u*, *luxu*, PS.-CYPR. *Sodom.* 44.

§54 **1.8** Certain nouns changed gender, *camelus*, f. (earlier in Pliny); *compes*, m., VVLG., LACT.; *cuculla*, f., HIER.; *testum*, n., ITAL., SVLP.-SEV.

§55 **1.9** Changes of declension:
1.9.1 first instead of third, *retia*, f., for *rete*, ITAL., FVLG.
1.9.2 second instead of third, *altarium*, beside *altare*; *ossum*, for *os*, ITAL., TERT.
1.9.3 second instead of fourth, *grados*.
1.9.4 third instead of second, *diacon* and *diaconus*.
§§ In the Middle Ages, numerous neuter plurals became feminine singulars in *-a*; even earlier one encounters these feminines: *spolia*, AVG. Serm. 146, 1 (Mai); *folia*, ISID. Or. 17, 9, 105; *examina*, VICT.-VIT. 1, 23.
Note also these variants: *unanimus* and *unanimis*, *exanimus* and *exanimis*.

§56 **1.10** Certain singulars are rare or not in use in Classical Latin: *altare, uirgultum, cunabulum, fomentum, tenebra, etc.*

§§57 **1.11** Some writers created comparatives by starting from the superlative forms:

nouissimiora, PASS. PERP. 1, 'the most recent' (opposed to nouitiora 'more recent, recent')
proximior, IREN. 1, 8, 5; CASS. Var. 11, 36;
maximior, HIER. Tr. I in psal. p. 310, 1.

Most of these forms were not admitted into the language of educated people.

§58 **1.12** The nominative *uestri* is sometimes found instead of *uos*: CASS., CAES.-AREL.

§§59 **1.13** Some aberrant forms like *illo* for *illi*; *illum* for *illud*; *ipsud*; *alium* for *aliud*; gen. f. *aliae*; dat. *alio, etc.*

2 Conjugation

§60 **2.1** *Fui, fueram, fuero, fuerim, fuissem, fuisse* are often used for *sum, eram, ero, sim, essem, esse,* in the compound tenses of the passive or of deponent verbs, without change of meaning:

narrauit se datum fuisse Manichaeis, AVG. Conf. 3, 12;
neque fuerint accusati, Parm. 1, 3, 4;
qui ausi fuerunt dissoluere, DION.-EX. (Ma. 2, c. 1321).

§61 **2.2** The archaic and poetic forms in *-arier, -irier* are found in Arnobius, Prudentius, and even after them: *conuestirier,* ARN. 5, 41; *uelarier, ibid.* 5, 7.

§62 **2.3** The verb *odi* is often found conjugated like *odio, odire*: VVLG., TERT., HIER., etc.

Analogous anomalies in compounds with *eo, exiet, exiebam, transiet, etc.*

§63 **2.4** Changes of conjugation: *extergĕ̆re, abstergĕ̆re,* for *extergēre, abstergēre; indulgeam,* SID. Ep. 4, 24, for *indulgebo; respondeam,* AVG. Serm. (Morin p. 133, 15), for *respondebo; cupiret,* PASS. PERP. 3, for *cuperet.* See also the chapter on the subjunctive.

§64 **2.5** Deponent verbs are frequently used with a passive meaning, the deponent verbs having taken the active form; or, less often, active verbs have taken a deponent form, and some impersonal verbs are used as personal verbs.

§65 **2.6** Some present participles are used adjectivally in the superlative and with a passive meaning, by a kind of confusion with the gerundive:

desiderantissimus, AVG. Ep. 67; 25, 2; CYPR. Ep. 4, 5, etc., 'very worthy of affection',

or by confusion with the passive past participle:

conclamantissimus, ALCIM. (Peip. p. 60), 'the most famous'.

§§66 **2.7** Certain cases of tmesis are unknown in classical literature:

qui in hisdem diebus tantae sollennitati inter non fuerit, PEREG. 49, 2;
pseudo quo christiana, VEREC. Cant. Eccl. 2, 5;
nihil esse debet inter, LVCIF. p. 3, 8.

Syntax

The syntax of Late Latin could be summed up in one line: 'There is not a classical rule which has not been violated.'

That is how a purist would express himself. But today we no longer have the 'classical' prejudice, and we know that languages evolve. That the Christian writers speak the language of their time is not a fault. What is a fault and allows one to call that period 'decadent' is the grammatical anarchy and uncertainty, a fault which one notices especially in the second- and third-rate writers. A writer cannot be called decadent because he uses the indicative instead of the subjunctive in an indirect question if that use has become habitual, hence normal and 'regular' in a way. But he deserves the description 'decadent' in so far as, for example, he sometimes uses one mood, sometimes another, under absolutely similar conditions, or if he confuses the usage of the demonstrative pronouns and indifferently uses one for the other. The precision instrument which a language ought to be has then deteriorated. In spite of the abandonment of most of the classical uses, the educated writers—and to the extent that they were educated—knew how to maintain a tradition, even in the Middle Ages; and so it is an Augustinian syntax, if not Ciceronian.

1 Use of Cases

1 Nominative

§§67 **1.1** Certain nominatives are either 'in the air,' used in an absolute way, by a sort of anacoluthon, or the word in the nominative will be related to a word in the sentence.[23]

nouiter *ueniens quis* ad conuersationem non *ei* facilis tribuatur ingressus, Ben. *Reg. 32*, 'if anyone suddenly presents himself for the monastic life, let him not be readily accepted';

pendebant quin immo circa eos anxia uota ciuitatis, *crescens* supra priuatos publicus *amor*, CASS. Var. 3, 5, 4, '... the public interest causing one to forget private feelings';

malens spiritus Dei dicere...(and another subject follows), GELAS. Tr. 3, 2;

benedicens nos episcopus, profecti sumus, PEREG. 16, 7 (cf. chap. 12, 7).

§68 **1.2** Example of exclamatory nominative:

o artis inaestimabilis uirtus! CASS. Var. 1, 45, 9.

2 Vocative

§69 In Later Latin, and not only in the Christian writers, participles are used in the vocative:

o ipse inuisus...et comprehense, ARN. 1, 31;

moriture, FORT. 4, 15;

and in the same way gerundives:

meritos inter commemorande uiros, AVS. 199, 6.

---

[23] We show in small print, more often than in a comment, the grammatical characteristics which seem to be uncommon. [In this translation these sections have not been printed in smaller letters but have been indicated by two section signs, e.g. §§67. In some cases only a paragraph is in small characters; each such paragraph is marked with a §§.]

3 Accusative

§70 **3.1** As in Plautus, certain objects [*compléments d'objet*] depend on a noun [i.e. in the examples below, function as direct objects of nouns of agency (AG 236)]:

pristi*num* doctor, TERT. Prax. 1, 'he who teaches ancient doctrine';
aduen*tum* praecursorem, OROS. Apol. 16, 2, 'who has preceded the coming';

or depend on an adjective with a verbal root, this being considered as a participle (*ignarus*, in Classical Latin, can be constructed with an infinitive clause or an indirect question):

dispersionis exi*tum* querulus, TERT. Res. 31;
tam necessarium absen*tiam* eius impatiens, Scorp. 3.

§71 **3.2** The accusative of specification [synechdochial or Greek Accusative, AG 397b, GL 338], in imitation of the Greek, is more prevalent than in Classical Latin, either with an intransitive verb:

caput meum doleo, VVLG. 4 Reg. 4, 19;
cum *oculum* grauiter dolere coepisset, SVLP.-SEV. Mart. 19, 3;

or especially with a passive verb (cf. Classical Latin *indutus*):

aeratus crepi*dam*, TERT. Pall. 4, 'shod in bronze';
exutus sto*lam* nuptialem, VICT.-VIT. 3, 36;
in me ocu*los* tuos fixus es, CYPR. Ad. Don. 1;
a daemone potata est obliuionis medicamen*tum*, IREN. 2, 33, 2, 'the demon made him drink the medicine of forgetfulness';
quae mandatus est a Patre, TERT. Prax. 8, 'that with which the Father has charged him';

or after a noun and having the force of a modifier indicating quality [*complément de qualité*]:

ceteris *hoc genus* pestibus, AVG. Ord. 2, 4, 12 (= *eiusdem generis*).

§72 **3.3** Double accusative, with verbs other than *doceo, rogo, celo, etc.*;

expoliantes *uos* ueterem hominem, VVLG. Col. 3, 9, 'stripping yourself of the old man';
calcia *te* caligas tuas, Act. 12, 8;
induit enim *me* indumen*tum* salutaris, TERT. Marc. 4, 11 (cf. no. 4);
hoc commemorat Iudaeos, AVG. Serm. (Morin p. 148, 20), 'he mentions it' (calls it to mind) to the Jews';
procul positos ueneni ui*rus* infundat, VICT.-VIT. 2, 37;
exigere aliquem aliquid, CASS. Var. 11, praef.

and with a passive:

cib*ari* eos *panem* lacrymarum, PASS. VII MON. 5;

exor*ati* ius*tum*, CASS. Var. 2, 27, 'as they had demanded of them what is just'.

§73 **3.4** Accusative of the same meaning or of the same root as the verb, with or without an adjective or determinative:

iudicare iniquitatem, VVLG. Ps. 81, 2, 'to pronounce an iniquitous judgement';
qui non loquimur magna, sed uiuimus, CYPR. Bon. pat. 3, 'we whose greatness is not in our high-sounding words, but in our acts';
Tyrus sabbatizauit sabbata sua, HIER. Ez. 9, 29, 8;
cf. nec a me totae (noctes) dormiuntur, AVG. Ep. 13, 1.

§74 **3.5** Accusative as a direct object [*complément de objet*] with some verbs which in Classical Latin are intransitives or are constructed with the the dative or the ablative:

fructificet terra herbam, TERT. Herm. 29 (Gen. 1, 11);
praeuaricare caerimonias, VVLG. Leu. 5, 15, 'to transgress the ceremonies';
exire ianuam, Mat. 26, 71;
exire domum, HIER. Ep. 22, 25;
praeuaricare mandatum, C. Pelag. 3, 6;
ne molle otium consuescant, Cass. Var. 1, 24.

See other examples in the dictionary under the words *careo, indigeo, utor, etc.*

§75 **3.6** In the accusative of place [*accusatif complément de lieu*], one finds—in contrast to Classical Latin usage—some names of countries without a preposition:

perrexit Aethiopiam, HIER. Ep. 53, 1;

and inversely some names of towns with a preposition:

uenit iterum in Cana Galilaeae, VVLG. Io. 4, 46.

§76 **3.7** Vulgar Latin does not distinguish between the idea of place where one is and the idea of place to which one goes (*in mentem esse* PL.). Late Latin quite often confuses them. Examples of this are found in the dictionary, especially with the preposition *in*:

christianos esse in causam, TERT. Apol. 40;
in insulis relegamur, Apol. 12;
iacent in sepulcra, HIER. Tr. I in psal. p. 66, 15.

§§77a **3.8** The accusative absolute appears only at a relatively late time:

machinis constructis *omnia*que *genera* tormentorum *adhibita*, IORD. (Momm. p. 119);

quinque psalmi...repetantur...lectionum uel uersuum *dispositionem* uniformem cunctis diebus *seruatam*, BEN. Reg. 18.

Others, e.g. in LVCIF., GREG.-T., ENNOD.

§§77b **3.9** In inscriptions, in writings of a popular nature, and in very late writers, one finds the accusative after some prepositions which normally govern the ablative, like *sine, pro, de,* and *cum*; see examples in the dictionary.

§§78 **3.10** Certain proper nouns are used as invariable nouns in the accusative:

in uilla *Cellas* nominala (Bonnet, p. 571, note);
in castello quod *Nouas* dicitur, GREG.-M. Ep. 9, 155, p. 155, 22;
cf. *Vitas* patrum Emeritensium, which seems to be a Hispanicism.

§§79 **3.11** Accusative confused with the nominative:

festiuitates sunt et *missas*, CONC. MEROV. p. 127, 7;
dum *missas* dicuntur, p. 181, 14.

4 Genitive

The uses that we are about to review, with the exception of the Hebraisms and the Hellenisms (the genitive of comparison [*génitif complément du comparatif*] and the genitive absolute), also belong to Classical Latin; but Late Latin and Christian writers in particular are distinguished by a greater boldness in their use of them.

§80 **4.1** Objective genitive:

persecutio *nostri*, CYPR. Ep. 52, 2, 'the persecution against us';
ueritatis error, Mort. 1, 'deviation far from the truth';
promissiones *patrum*, Rom. 15, 8, 'the promises made to our fathers';
commutationem *Christi*, Ps. 88, 52, 'the change with respect to your anointed';
potestates *spirituum* immundorum, Mat. 10, 1, 'the power over unclean spirits';
sine ulla *sui* contumelia, AVG. Bapt. 2, 1, 2 (= *erga se*);
Dei reprehensio, Praedest. 8, 16, 'reproach made to God';
ad *Dei* deuotionem, PS.-AVG. Qu. test. 47, 3;
fundi controuersia, CASS. Var. 1, 5, 'disagreement concerning an estate'.

§81 **4.2** Subjective genitive:

caritas *Dei* ad hominem, SERM. ARR. FRG. 2, 10;
absentia *nostri*, HIER. Ep. 127, 8. (See other examples in the personal pronouns, 4.3.)

§82 **4.3** Explanatory genitive or genitive of identity [cf. L 1255-57 and GL 361]:

sacramentum *infanticidii*, TERT. Apol. 7, 'the rite of infanticide';
baptismum *paenitentiae*, VVLG. Luc. 3, 3;
fici arbor, Mat. 24, 32;
arbores *rosae*, PASS. PERP. 11;
sycomori arbor, AVG. Serm. 113, 3;
arbores *citriorum*, C. Faust. 21, 12, 'lemon trees';
osculum *pacis*, Serm. 204, 1;
proelium *tentationis*, Serm. 210, 2;
Deus *misericordiarum*, Conf. 5, 9;
omni *humilitatis* subiectione, BEN. Reg. 3;
pietatis remedium, CASS. Var. 4, 41;
paralysis *peccatorum*, CAES.-AREL. Serm. (Morin p. 273, 27), 'the paralysis due to sin'.

The Spanish style loves the redundancies of this type of genitive:

iniquitatum facinora, MOZAR. Sacram. p. 364;
dilectio caritatis, p. 231;
mandatorum praecepta, p. 842;
cf. ira indignationis, VVLG. Ps. 77, 45.

Examples of the explanatory genitive of time:

post mille annos *mortis suae*, LACT. Inst. 7, 22, 8;
annus sextus *depositionis suae*, EVGIPP. Vit. Seu. 44, 6;
ante annos Vrbis conditae MCCC, OROS. Hist. 1, 4, 1.

§83 **4.4** Genitive of origin [cf. L 1232]:

laetitiae *salutaris* tui, VVLG. Ps. 50, 13, 'the joy from your salvation';
uerba *pectoris*, HIER. Ep. 22, 7;
uirgo Dauidicae *stirpis*, LEO-M. Serm. 21;
dolor *filiorum*, PS.-AVG. Qu. test. 127, 30, 'the grief which comes from sons';
Indici *maris* conchae, CASS. Var. 1, 35.

§84 **4.5** Genitive of appurtenance, meaning 'son of' (Classical Latin), 'husband of, slave of, widow of, etc.' (a Hellenism):

Iuda *Simonis*, VVLG. Io. 6, 71;
Maria *Cleophae*, Io. 19, 25, 'the wife of Cleophas' (ἡ τοῦ Κλωπᾶ);
Paula *Toxitii*, HIER. Ep. 107, 13, 'widow of Toxitius';
cf. *Christi* esse 'to be of Christ, to belong to him'.

§85 **4.6** The genitive of quality occurs more frequently than the ablative:

homines *bonae voluntatis*, VVLG. Luc. 2, 14;
Deus...patiens et *multae misericordiae*, Ps. 85, 14;
uir *bonae memoriae*, CYPR. Ep. 71, 4;

this last expression often modifies a proper noun: CASS., GREG.-M., etc.;

homo *totius iustitiae*, LVCIF. Moriend. 12;

homines uel *mediocris intelligentiae*, CASS. Var. 12, 5.

The genitive of quality, not modified by an epithet, is equivalent to an adjective. It was found earlier in the work of Plautus, Catullus, and the postclassical writers (cf. *homo iustus et morum*, APUL.). It was widely developed under the influence of Latin translations of the Bible.

mons *sanctificationis*, VVLG. Ps. 77, 54, 'holy mountain';

uiri *sanguinum*, Ps. 25, 9, 'sanguinary men';

uiri *diuitiarum*, P.-NOL. Ep. 34, 4;

uas *electionis*, CYPR. Hab. uirg. 23 and VVLG., 'elected vessel, chosen vessel' (when speaking of a person);

cibum *salutis*, Dom. orat. 18;

spiritus *uirtutis*, VVLG. Sap. 5, 24, 'violent wind';

ciuitas *sanguinum*, HIER. Ep. 53, 8;

homo *potestatis*, PETIL. ap. AVG. C. litt. Petil. 4, 31, 70, 'a powerful person';

oculus *carnis*, Conf. 6, 16, 'the carnal eye';

Dominus *gloriae*, Serm. 213, 3;

iniquitatis uiri, AMBR. Ep. 5, 19;

Deus *maiestatis*, FORT. Carm. 11, 1, 19;

uita *duplicitatis*, GREG.-M. Moral. 9, 49, 85;

in actione *praecipitationis*, ibid. 1, 25, 35;

puritatis deuotione, BEN. Reg. 20 (= *pura deuotione*);

cf. with preposition, homo de ciuitate, VIT. PATR. 6, 3, 15, 'a city-dweller'.

§§86 **4.7** Genitive in place of a predicate noun:

cui *artis* erat uestimenta componere, GREG.-T. Mart. 2, 58, 'whose craft was to make clothes';

nobis *consuetudinis* est ut, PEREG. 10, 7, 'it is our custom to'.

§87 **4.8** Augmentative genitive; although it was not unknown in secular literature (κακὰ κακῶν, SOPH. Oed. Col. 1238; *uictor uictorum*, PL. Trin. 309), it is primarily a Hebraism:

super caelum caeli, VVLG. Ps. 67, 34, 'to the highest part of the heavens';

caeli caelorum, 3 Reg. 8, 27;

uanitas uanitatum, Eccl. 1, 2;

millia millium, Apoc. 5, 12;

Dominus dominorum, rex regum, ibid, 17, 14;

sublimitates sublimitatum, TERT. Val. 7.

§88 **4.9** Genitive of material in place of an adjective or in place of *ex* with the ablative:

ferri circulum, HIER. Ep. 7, 3;

statua *salis*, In Is. 16, 57, 7;
cf. oculus *carnis*, AVG. Conf. 6, 16.

§§Certain explanatory genitives specify the nature of a place:
lapidum loca, VICT.-VIT. 2, 36;
loca *siluarum*, ibid. 1, 37 (1, 11) (= *loca siluosa*).

§89 **4.10** Genitive of cause, with verbs other than *condemno, accuso, etc.*:
criminis *cuius* impetuntur, CASS. Var. 4, 23;
cuius *meriti* sepultus, SVLP.-SEV. Mart. 11, 4.

§90 **4.11** Genitive with adjectives [*génitif complément d'adjectifs*] which in Classical Latin are not constructed with this case (e.g. with *dignus*, poetic in Classical Latin):
dignum *tantae feminae* habitaculum, HIER. Ep. 77, 8;
digni *Dei* caelorum, COMM. Apol. 664;
exsul *paradisi*, HIER. Iou. 2, 15;
exsul *pectoris tui*, AVG. Serm. 311, 13;
mendaciorum loquacissimus, TERT. Apol. 16;
aurium caeci, An. 10;
infirmo...*dominandi*, Adu. Marc. 4, 21;
ingratus *beneficiorum Dei*, HIER. Is. 18 pr.;
promptus *disserendi*, SVLP.-SEV. Chron. 2, 46, 3;
conscius *sui*, CASS. Var. 11, praef.

§91 **4.12** Topographical genitive in place of a noun in apposition (*urbem Pataui*, CATVL.; *lacus Auerni*, VIRG.):
in *Iordanis* flumine, VVLG. Marc. 1, 5;
ad flumen *Iordanis*, AVG. Serm. 288, 2;
oppidum *Stridonis*, HIER. Vir. ill. 135;
cf. in Thebaidis locis, VIT. PATR. 7, 19, 3, c. 1044A.

§92 **4.13** Names of countries used in the locative:
Palestinae, HIER. Vit. Hil. 44, in Palestine.

§§93 **4.14** Genitive of place, which can be explained by an ellipsis or by the absence of the article [pronoun-adjective *is*, cf. §131]:
Bellonae (*templum* understood) TERT. Pall. 4;
in Regnorum (*libris* understood), Iud. 13;
Cata Pauli (*domum* understood), AGAP. II (M. 133, c. 916A).

§94 **4.15** Genitive of comparison [*génitif complément du comparatif*] (a Hellenism):
maiorem *Asiae* et *Africae* terram, TERT. Apol. 40, 'land greater than Asia and Africa';

angeli inferiores *Dei*, Carn. Chr. 3;
maiora *horum* audiuit auris mea, VVLG. Eccli. 16, 6;
maiora *horum* uidebitis, IREN. 4, 9, 2;
omnium maior, HIER. Ep. 108, 3;
maior *messorum*, AVG. Parm. 1, 14, 21;
fortior *omnium*, PS.-AVG. Qu. test. 92, 1.

In examples such as the last example above or in examples like this—*cum sis* omnium *minor*, VIT. PATR. 5, 10, 28—it seems that the comparative is being confused with the superlative; cf. omnium artium *innocentior*, ARN.-I. c. 603B.

§§95 **4.16** Also a Hellenism is the genitive as the object of verbs [*génitif complément d'objet*] such as *audio*, ITAL. Dan. 9, 6, ap. CYPR. Laps. 31; *dominor*, TERT. Apol. 26 and AVG. Ciu. 20, 9.

§§96 **4.17** Examples of the genitive absolute are rare; some are doubtful or seem to be the result of the translator's carelessness:

cogitantium omnium, ITAL. Luc. 3, 15 (διαλογιζομένων πάντων);
inter se inuicem cogitationum accusantium, Rom. 2, 15 (VVLG. *cogitationibus)*, 'the diversity of opinions accusing them';
extremae confusionis non habentis propriam substantiam, IREN. 2, 7, 1, 'extreme confusion and without proper existence' [her last state of confusion not having substance of its own];
cf. uidentibus quingentis uiris...et omnium apostolorum, HIER. (Morin, *Études* I, p. 250).

§97 **4.18** Genitive with a noun [*génitif complément du nom*] when a dative with the verb was expected:

ad fidem *illius* abrogandam, ARN. 3, 1;
si tantam curam *instructionis* nostrae insumpsit Spiritus Sanctus, TERT. Herm. 22;
comites *homicidii* adiungere, PASS. PERP. 21;
ille tunc imber...mortem intulit *corporum*, INTERP. IO.-CHRYS. Hom. 7, 7;
ibi accessus Romanorum non est. PEREG. 20, 12.

§98 **4.19** Genitive in place of *in* or *ad* with the accusative:

ante litoris exitum, AVG. C. part. Don. 10, 14, 'before the departure at the shore'.

5 Dative

Listed below are the principal uses to keep in mind, apart from constructions that are peculiar to a particular verb or adjective, which will be found in the dictionary:

§99 **5.1** The dative of interest is extended to indicate the purpose, the direction, or that towards which the soul tends (a similar use was seen earlier in Vergil and Tacitus):

psallam *nomini tuo*, VVLG. Ps. 7, 18;
cf. exultare *Domino*, iubilare *Deo* (frequent in the Psalms);
mundo periit et *Christo* reuixit, HIER. Ep. 38, 12;
modo nati sunt *Christo*, qui prius nati fuerant *saeculo*, AVG. Serm. 228, 1.

You should notice also: peccaui *tibi*, Ps. 40, 4, 'I have sinned against you'; qui bene *nobis meriti* fuerint, CASS. Var. 5, 27, in place of *de nobis*.

Mihi can be used in place of *meus*:

nunc ad te *mihi* omnis dirigitur oratio, HIER. Ep. 22, 15;
filius mihi mortuus est, Tr. II in psal. p. 92, 1;
ad te ergo nunc *mihi* sermo dirigitur, BEN. Reg. prol.;
cf. mulieri quae volebat illi tangere pedes, AVG. Serm. 5, 7 (= *eius*).

§§Close to the dative of interest are the expletive datives, which seem to belong to Vulgar Latin:

sedete *uobis*, PEREG. 36, 5;
gustauimus *nobis*, ibid. 4, 8, 'we ate some food';
ambulauimus *nobis* per heremum, ANTON. Itin. 36;
tu te *tibi* arbitraris contumeliam te pati, LVCIF., p. 251, 6 (see the chapter on personal pronouns, §170).

On the other hand, one finds earlier in the work of Plautus, Catullus, and Quintilian some datives of interest which designate the person who judges, and some are found in our writers:

nemo *Deo* pauper est, LACT. Inst. 5, 18, 'in the eyes of God';
qui *ceteris* deus, sibi certe homo est, MINVC. 29, 4.

§100 **5.2** The dative is found as a dative of agent [*complément d'agent*] after a passive verb, in place of the ablative (there are examples earlier in Plautus, Varo, and even Cicero):

commissa *sibi* flagitia, AMBR. Psal. 37, 2 (= *a se*);
singulis aequaliter colligebatur (manna), CYPR. Ep. 69, 14, 'each collected an equal part of it';
tanto episcoporum *numero* damnati sunt, AVG. Parm. 1, 11, 18 (in some examples, it can be interpreted as an ablative without a preposition);
consulibus pulli pascuntur, SALV. Gub. 6, 12;
quaesitus *aduersario* testis, MAMERT. St. an. 2, 9, p. 134;
huic igni mundatur, HIER. Tr. II in psal. p. 274, 12;
nihil dignum morte actum est *ei*, VVLG. Luc. 23, 15, 'he has not done anything which deserves death' (a Hellenism);
despectus *patri*, AMBR. Ep. 2, 24.

§§In the following example, the dative can be accounted for by assuming that the writer wanted a parallel construction:

Palaestinae interrogaris et respondes Aegypto, HIER. C. Ioan. 4, 'Palestine questions you, and it is to Egypt that you respond'.

§§One finds this dative-with-adjective construction:

omni regno desiderabilis esse debet tranquillitas, CASS. Var. 1, 1, 1.

§101 **5.3** Dative of gerundive expressing purpose in place of *ad* and the accusative:

mulcendis sensibus...hortorum facies amoena, CYPR. Ad Don. 1, 'the charming aspect of gardens, well suited to delight the senses'.

§102 **5.4** Dative of direction in place of *ad* and the accusative:

optate *tranquillitati* nauem perducere, AVG. Beat. uit. 1, 4;

libros *mihi* directos, HIER. Pachom. pr. (Classical Latin also uses the dative with *mitto*);

uniuersae *Africae* destinauit, VICT.-VIT. 2, 38, 'he traveled to all of Africa';

exilio trudebatur, ibid. 1, 22 (= *in exilium*);

(uasa) sacris *liminibus* deportari, CASS. Var. 12, 20.

§103 **5.5** Dative of place, even with simple verbs:

posui *ori meo* custodiam, VVLG. Ps. 38, 2 (= *imposui*);

quibus dominorum clementia noluit descendere, CASS. Var. 11, 16 (= *condescendere*).

§104 **5.6** Dative with adjectives [*datif complément d'adjectifs*] that do not admit this construction in Classical Latin:

exosam *Deo* superbiam, PS.-RVF. In Am. 6, 1;

dulcis erat *iusto principi* rationabilis contrarietas obsequentis, CASS. Var. 8, 9, 'the just prince gladly paid attention to the reasonable contradictoriness of a respected subject'.

§§105 **5.7** Dative with the comparative:

nullumque *sibi* asserebat esse prudentiorem, GREG.-T. Hist. 6, 46;

esto subditus et humilior *omni creaturae*, VIT. PATR. 5, 1, 8;

maiores *tibi* aut coaetanei, ibid. 5, 15, 76;

in the last examples, the dative can also be explained as governed by another nearby adjective which takes the dative.

§106 **5.8** *Est* with the dative sometimes means 'it pertains to, it is the distinctive feature of' (common in Classical Latin):

animae corporatae est per corpus sentire corporea, *eidemque* sine corpore uidere incorporea, MAMERT. St. an. 1, 23, 'the soul joined to a body feels, thanks to the body, material things', just as without the body it perceives the immaterial.

6 Ablative

§107 **6.1** As a result of the more and more frequent use of prepositions, the ablative occurs less often alone than in Classical Latin. Nevertheless, here are some examples of ablatives used without the preposition *a*, to express separation:

donis spiritualibus enudari, VEREC. Cant. 8, 1;
uacuabat alios labore, CASS. Var. 9, 24, 'he relieved others of their work'.

§108 **6.2** Ablative of place without the preposition *in*:

non orbis terrae *uno angulo* aedificabatur, AVG. Ep. 142, 2;
suis *separatis* conuenticulis congregantur, Parm. 1, 12, 19;
paruo oppido morabatur, EVGIPP. Vit. Seu. 1;
pulpito sistens, VICT.-VIT. 1, 41 (cf. 5.5).

§§It is even found in place of the locative: Epheso, VVLG. Apoc. 1, 11.

§109 **6.3** The adverbial ablative corresponds to a more extended use of the ablative of manner:

iniustitia, TERT. Herm. 11, 'unjustly';
uoluntate, CYPR. Ep. 56, 1, 'voluntarily', and also frequently in the work of AVG.;
uirgines carne, non spiritu, HIER. Ep. 22, 5, 'physically virgins, not morally'.

A great number of adverbial modifiers [*compléments circonstanciels*] incorporating the word *mente* usher in the formation of French adverbs in *-ment*:

sana mente putare, AVG. Ciu. 1, 18, 'reasonably' [*raisonnablement*];
simplici mente pensare, AMBR. Hex. 2, 1, 3;
firma mente tenere, HIER. Ephes. 3, 5, 4;
intrepida mente respondebo, Orig. Luc. hom. 35, 'boldly' [*hardiment*];
fera mente, COMM. Instr. 1, 28, 24, 'savagely' [*sauvagement*].

§110 **6.4** Ablative of duration in place of the accusative:

manebit paucis diebus, HIER. Pachom. 49;
mansi apud eum diebus quindecim, VVLG. Gal. 1, 18;
multo tempore iacuit, VICT.-VIT. 1, 40;
lecturus tota hebdomada, BEN. Reg. 48, 'he who is obliged to read for an entire week'.

§111 **6.5** Ablative of agent with a noun [*ablatif complément d'agent avec un nom*]:

uastationem totius barbaro *hoste* prouinciae, HIER. Ep. 118, 2.

§112 **6.6** Ablative of measure in place of the accusative [AG 423, 425]: latus est duobus pedibus, MAMERT. St. an. 1, 20.

§113 **6.7** Ablative of the gerundive dependent on an adjective:
conspiciendo Deo digni, CYPR. Ep. 6, 1, 'worthy of seeing God'.

§114 **6.8** Ablative absolute referring to the subject of the sentence:
qui se possunt *monitore* compelli, CASS. Var. 7, 26;
quos a discipulis suis, *sese hic constituto* ('in his presence'), *maluit* baptizari, AVG. Ep. ad cath. 21, 58;
quibus pergentibus audiunt, GREG.-T. Hist. 3, 15, 'by going there they learn' (see the syntax of the participle, Ch. 12, 6).

§115 **6.9** Ablative absolute of the type *Cicerone consule*, with nouns other than those found in Classical Latin:
adhuc *diacono* Caeciliano, AVG. Breu. coll. 3, 12, 24.
Ablative absolute with a subject understood:
non solum non faciebamus, sed nec facientibus (understood *eis*) tacebamus, Parm. 3, 4, 23,'... but furthermore, when they did it, we did not keep silent'.

§116 **6.10** Ablative with the superlative [*ablatif complément du superla-tif*], through confusion of the comparative with the superlative and of the weakening of their respective meanings:
se omnibus sanctis (var. *ex omnibus*) infimum dicere, HIER. Ephes. 3, 8.

§117 In the dictionary one will find modifiers of comparatives [*compléments du comparatif*] with the prepositions *de, prae, super, extra, ultra,* and *inter*.

§§118 **6.11** Ablative of the name of a town in place of the accusative or the nominative:
Sicca Veneria et *Laribus* duas esse ciuitates, VICT.-VIT. 2, 22;
urbs *Laribus*, CORIPP. Ioh. 6, 143;
iuxta fluuium *Ira*, IORD. Get. 45;
cf. *Metis* 'Metz', an ancient ablative of *meta*, which became a nominative in the Merovingian period.

2 Prepositions

In the dictionary will be found new meanings of the different prepositions and also idioms formed from prepositions and adverbs. We should like simply to draw attention to the following particulars.

§119 **1.** There are numerous examples of prepositions that are not repeated (Varro and Vitruvius provide some earlier examples):

non in gymnasiis sed *igne* iaculati, TERT. Spect. 30;
propter humilitatis formam, *quam* (= propter quam) docendam uenerat docendam uenerat, AVG. Ep. 55, 18, 33;
secundum hanc pulchritudinem magis quam *corpus* (= secundum corpus) sumus ad imaginem Dei, Ep. 120, 4, 20;
in hac amentia, *qua* uiuis nunc, LVCIF. p. 317, 28;
de sermone, *quo* uertitur controuersia, AVELL. p. 200, 2;
ad causam, *quam* directus fuerit, CASS. Var. 4, 47, 4;
per...mansiones *quas* ueneramus, PEREG. 21, 5.

§120 **2.** Certain ellipses with prepositions can be accounted for by the absence of the article [the pronoun-adjective *is*, cf. §131]:

praeter in Spiritum Sanctum. PS.-AVG. Qu. test. 102, 12, 'except those (sins) against the Holy Spirit';
ex gentilibus iudaizare debere docebat, ibid. 60, 2, 'he was teaching those who came from paganism that they should adopt the Jewish rites';
de uirginis exire, TERT. Virg. uel. 8, 'to cease to be virginal' (τοῦ τῆς παρθένου ἐξιέναι);

for *de cuius* 'of the things of whom, of the matter of whom', see the dictionary under the word *qui*.[24]

[24] Analogous examples in Vulgar Latin in the sermons of St. Augustine: ergo de Dei das Deo, Serm. 168, 5: cf. 232, 4; Frangip. 1, 5.

§121 **3.** The poets of our period make use of, to a much greater extent than the classical poets, the metathesis that consists of placing the preposition after its object:

famulo sine, P.-NOL. Carm. 16, 286.

§122 **4.** The classical writers used certain ablatives, followed by a modifier in the genitive [*complément au génitif*], with the force of a preposition: *causa, gratia, beneficio, auxilio, arte, fraude, dolo, insidiis, consilio, uoce, etc.*

Our writers have extended this usage further:

aestimatione 'in consideration of'

dum..., meritorum aestimatione, penderemus incerto, ENNOD. Ep. 5, 3 (Vog. p. 183, 9) 'when our wrongdoings left us everything to fear (= pro meritis, says Vogel);

beneficio offers numerous examples in which the original meaning has completely disappeared:

aestus ualidus turbarum beneficio, PASS. PERP. 3, 'one suffocated there because of the crowd';

contemplatione 'in consideration of' (EVGIPP.), 'having regard to (LACT., AMBR.);

indultu, SID. 'thanks to';

intuitu, VLP., FORT., CASS., ADAM., 'with the intent of, by, for';

merito, LACT. VICT.-VIT., 'thanks to'; and even 'because of';

sanctorum merito, VICT.-VIT. 1, 35, 'because of the presence of the saints (the devils indulge in all sorts of evil spells) and so a purely causal sense;

ministerio, HILAR., ENNOD., 'by means of, thanks to';

sub obtentu, LACT., FORT., CYPR., 'under the pretext of';

obtentu, (1) 'while alleging, under the pretext of (SID.);
(2) 'for the purpose of, by' (SID.);
(3) 'in consideration of' (EVGIPP.);
(4) 'for the purpose of obtaining, for' (RER. MEROV.);

officio, ALCIM., 'through the agency of, thanks to';

opportunitate, ALCIM., 'thanks to';

cf. ad ostensionem, VICT.-VIT. 2, 9, 'before, in the view of, under the eyes of;

mulieres...ad ostensionem totius ciuitatis ducebantur, VICT.-VIT. 2, 9, (*ad* does not here express purpose);

in ostensione cunctorum, ibid. 3, 35.

Certain idioms correspond to Hebraisms: *in ore gladii,* Iudith 2, 16, 'on the edge of the sword, by the sword'; in particular those which are formed with the word *facies*: a facie, in faciem, etc., 'before, in front of':

a facie aquilonis, Ier. 1, 4, ap. HIER. ibid. (see the details in the dictionary).

§123 **5.** A prepositional phrase used as a modifier [*un complément avec préposition*] can replace *quam* depending on the comparative:

sapientior prae omnibus, HIER. Tr. I in psal. p. 165, 27;
melius...super diuitias, VVLG. Ps. 36, 16;
meliores super nos, VIT. PATR. 6, 1, 14;
potiores a scribis, LVCIF. Athan. 2, 5;
fortiora ab eis, CASS. Psal. 21, 20 (after a positive, see the next chapter).

3 Comparatives and Superlatives

§124 **1.** Positive in place of the comparative, or the use of a verb implying *magis*:

bonum est tibi in uitam intrare *quam* mitti in gehennam, VVLG. Mat. 18, 9, 'it is better for you...';
nihil est quod *indurat* mentes hominum *quam*, TERT. Bapt. 2;
candidi dentes eius *quam* lac, IREN. 4, 10, 2.

For the positives constructed with *prae* or *super,* in place of *quam*, see these prepositions in the dictionary, where phrases such as these will be found:

terribilis super omnes, VVLG. Ps. 88, 8;
inclytus prae fratribus suis, 1 Par. 4, 9.

Comparisons with the genitive [*génitif complément du comparatif*] were mentioned in Chap. 1, 4.15.

§125 **2.** Comparative in place of the positive:

manifestius est, CYPR. Ep. 67, 6, (= manifestum est) 'sufficiently manifest, manifest';
quos ipse fecerat *tristes*, laborauit reddere laetiores,CASS. Var. 3, 51.

Examples of postclassical pleonasms:

magis utilius, CYPR. Bon. pat. 1;
multo plus lucidiores, VVLG. Eccli. 23, 28;
magis mitior, CASS. Var. 5, 42 (cf. minus locupletior, Var. 11, 8);
omnibus amplius asperior, VIT. PATR. 3, 61 (see the word *maxime* in the dictionary).

§126 **3.** Comparative in place of the superlative:

sublimiora Spiritus Sancti charismata, CASSIAN. Coll. 1, 11, 1, 'the most sublime gifts...';
sapientior prae omnibus, HIER. Tr. I in psal. p. 165, 27;
unicuique patria sua carior est, CASS. Var. 1, 21;

quam plura, VICT.-VIT. 2, 64 (= quam plurima), 'the most possible, as many as possible'.

§127 **4.** Superlative in place of the comparative:
plurimam hostiam Abel *quam* Cain obtulit Deo, VVLG. Hebr. 11, 4, 'offered to God a victim superior to that of Cain';
tanto diuinitati *plurima* debemus, *quanto* a ceteris mortalibus *maiora* suscipimus, CASS. Var. 8, 24 (Classical Latin tanto plura) 'the more we receive...the more we are obliged...'

§128 **5.** Periphrastic comparatives and superlatives:
5.1 Comparative:
magis bonus, VVLG. Sap. 8, 20;
quanto magis grata est, CASS. Var. 6, 15;
even before a superlative:
magis proxima, TERT. Apol. 23.
Especially with the adverb *plus* (postclassical Latin):
plus humilis, HIER. Ep. 22, 27;
cf. RVF. Interp. Ios. 4, 2; P.-PETRIC. Mart. 6, 112; IGNAT. Ep. ad Polyc. 3, 2;
§§The last can be in correlation with *magis:*
quanto plus se deiciebat, tanto magis a Christo subleuabatur, HIER. Ep. 108, 3.
With *nimis* 'more':
nimis imbecillum et fragilem *quam*, LACT. Opif. 3, 1;
(redundancy) acerbius nimis, AVG. Conf. 8, 11;
nimis propius, LACT. Opif. 9, 2.
With *satis* 'too':
OROS. Apol. 8, 1; VIT. PATR. 5,18, 19.
Phrase replacing a comparative:
supra solitum hiems sicca, CASS. Var. 12, 25, 5.

§129 **5.2** Superlative (already in colloquial Latin with the words *multum, satis, bene, fortiter, etc.*; in Vulgar Latin with *bene, probe, recte, infinitum, ingens,* and *insanum*);
with *multum* (PL., PLIN.-I.):
multum mirabilis, AVG. Ep. 187, 21;
multum tardus, Doct. chr. 4, 8, 22;
beatus multumque felix, HIER. Gal. 1, 2, 20; 3, 5, 13;
multum religiosus, BED. Hist. 4, 22;
even before a superlative:
multum carissime, AVG. Ep. 185, 44;
with *nimis* 'very, greatly' (rare in Classical Latin):
nimis sapientibus uiris, AVG. Ep. 161, 2;

cf. LACT. Mort. 40, 2; CYPR. Ep. 21, 4;

before a verb:

in mandatis eius volet nimis, VVLG. Ps. 111, 1;

to reinforce a superlative:

pulcherrima nimis, CASS. Compl. 20 in 1 Cor;

with *satis* 'very, quite':

cf. CYPR. Ep. 54, 2; 64, 1; SALV. Gub. 1, 2; 4, 4; MAMERT.St.an. 1, 2; 2, 7; 3, 1;

with *ualde* 'thoroughly, very':

gaudio magno ualde, VVLG. Mat. 2, 10;
ualde uelociter, Ps. 6, 11 (and often in the Vulgate);
ualde mirabile, AVG. Conf. 12, 18;
bona ualde, ibid. 13, 28; In Psal. 118, 4, 1;

even with a superlative:

ualde obscurissimus, HIER. Ep. 71, 7;
ualde pessime, AVG. C. litt. Petil. 3, 46, 56;

redundancy copied from Hebrew:

bonas bonas ualde, VVLG. Ier. 24, 3;
ualde ualde bona est, Num. 14, 7, ap. AVG. Locut. Num. 38;
ualde ualde inualescebat, Ex. 1, 7, ap. AVG. Locut. Exod. 1; cf. Ciu. 16, 26;

with *maxime*:

maxime desideranter, CASS. Var. 1, 4.

§130 **6.** Contrary to classical usage, writers coordinate adjectives and adverbs of a different degree:

boni et fidelissimi contubernales, MINVC. 1;
fortibus et ualidissimis, ARN. 2, 57;
quid est quod in hac parte aut uos *plurimum* habeatis aut nos *minus*? ibid. 2, 11;
meliores et humiles, BEN. Reg. 2.

4 Pronouns and Pronominal Adjectives

1 Absence of the article

§131 We have already mentioned, in sections 6, 27, 84, and 120, ways of expressing oneself which can be explained by the absence of the article [pronoun-adjective *is*].[25]

Here, moreover, are some adverbial modifiers [*compléments circonstan-ciels*] governed by a noun which can be explained in the same way:

inter se dissensiones, TERT. Ad mart. 1 (αἱ πρὸς ἀλλήλους διαφοραί);

secundum substantiam dissimilitudinem praedicabat, CASS. Hist. 6, 25 (τὸ κατ' οὐσίαν ἀνόμοιον, SOCR. 3, 10), 'he professes non-consubstantiality (anomoeism [the teachings of the Anomoeans]);

cf. tanquam impii et qui *illorum sapiunt* (τὰ ἐκείνων), LVCIF. p. 338, 8, and those who think as they do'.

2 Demonstratives

2.1 General remarks

§132 **2.1.1** Pleonastic uses of *ille, ipse*, and above all *is*, principally in the Psalms:

beatus *cuius* Deus Iacob adiutor *eius*, VVLG. Ps. 145, 5 (see also the relative pronouns);

et sepulcra *eorum* domus *illorum* in aeternum, Ps. 48, 11;

et exiui *ad eum* et aperui *ei*, PASS. PERP. 10;

---

[25] The following expressions are Hebraisms: *benedicite Deo Domino, de fontibus Israel*, VVLG. Ps. 67, 27, 'Oh, you who are descended from the sources of Israel'; cf. *ex illis occidetis*, Mat. 23, 34, 'you will kill some of them'; *quem appretiauerunt a filiis Israel*, Mat. 27, 9, 'whom thus certain sons of Israel had prized'. The reader will see later some demonstratives and relatives which correspond to a Greek article.

carnalis *concupiscentiae* ipsas *eius* amaritudines amamus, GREG.-M. Hom. eu. 28, 3;
fluuius autem quartus *ipse* est Euphrates, VVLG. Gen. 2, 14;
idem ipse propheta, BEN. Reg. 5 (in Classical Latin, *ipse* is used with another demonstrative to emphasize it: *is ipse* 'that very one');
persequuntur *ecclesiam* et *populantur illam*, HIER. Gal. 1, 1, 13.

§133 **2.1.2** Demonstrative corresponding to the Greek article:
principes *huius* populi, ITAL. Act. 4, 8 (ἄρχοντες τοῦ λαοῦ);
hi decem, ITAL. Luc. 17, 17 (οἱ δέκα);
excitauit Dominus satanam ipsi (τῷ) Salomoni, CYPR. Orat. 19 (Ital. 1 Reg. 11, 14);
respondit *ille* homo, VVLG. Io. 9, 30;
huic Dauid, Ps. 96.1, 'to David';
hi tales, BEN. Reg. 5 (οἱ τοιοῦτοι);
hanc eandem apocalypsim, VICT.-POETOV. p. 94, 1 (τὴν αὐτήν);
hos eosdem, ibid. p. 110, 9 (τοὺς αὐτούς); for id ipsum (τὸ αὐτό) see below [§163];
de hoc ipso, BARNAB. Ep. 4 (περὶ τοῦ αὐτοῦ);
cf. in hoc ut...uiuat. AVG. Ep. 164, 4, 10 (ITAL.) (εἰς τὸ...βιῶσαι).

§134 **2.1.3** As early as the end of the Empire, just as in the Middle Ages, *dictus, iam dictus, supra memoratus, praedictus, praefatus,* and similar expressions were used with almost the same meaning as *idem* 'the aforesaid'.

§135 **2.1.4** In Classical Latin, *is* is the usual antecedent of *qui*; in Late Latin, it can be replaced by any demonstrative:
per *ipsam quam* uicerat, LEO-M. Serm. 21, 1;
ab *his quos* lacessunt, MAMERT. St. an. 1, 1;
ex *his quae* uidit, ibid. 1, 24;
hi quibus commissum est, CASS. Var. 10, 28 (the Classical writers furnish examples of *hic* as an antecedent of *qui*, but in their works ordinarily *hic qui* states precisely, "this who [or this which]";
illud quod istā paginā propalatur, MAMERT. St. an. 1, 2.

§136 **2.1.5** *Is* tends to disappear, replaced by *hic, ille, ist,* and *ipse.*

§137 **2.1.6** The ancient distinction among the demonstratives, giving each personal connotations (i.e. *hic*, first person; *iste*, second person; and *ille*, third person) disappeared little by little. The demonstratives, *ipse* included, tend to be used indifferently, one for the other.

2.2 *Hic*

§138 **2.2.1** In the Old Latin versions of the Bible and in the Vulgate, the demonstrative *hic* is often joined to the word *mundus*:

in *hunc mundum* uenisti, VVLG. Io. 11, 27;
ab elementis *huius mundi*, ITAL. Col. 2, 20, ap. AVG. Ep. 149, 28.

§139 **2.2.2** *Hic* is used in place of *iste* (second person and with a pejorative connotation):

quae *haec* est insatiabilis carnificinae *rabies*? CYPR. Ad Demetr. 13.

§140 **2.2.3** *Hic ... hic*, in place of *hic...ille* 'the one...the other':

hunc humiliat, *hunc* exaltat, VVLG. Ps. 14, 8.

§141 **2.2.4** As in French, the neuter can call to mind an adjective:

iniusti sunt barbari, et nos *hoc* sumus, SALV. Gub. 4, 14, 65.

§142 **2.2.5** *Ille...hic*, in place of *hic...ille*:

nonnihil in *anima* humana esse *Deo* simile, quia sit *ille* lumen illuminans, et *haec* lumen illuminabile, MAMERT. St. an. 2, 2, p. 103, 9 (*ille* indicating here the nearest term).

2.3 *Idem*

§143 **2.3.1** Used in place of *ipse*:

in *eisdem* arboribus templi, TERT. Apol. 9;
eadem hora, PASS. AVR. p. 760, 'at the very hour' (*ipse* will quite often be seen in place of idem).

§144 **2.3.2** In place of *is*:

idem qui, LACT. Inst. 1, 1, 3;
eidem in notitiam perferatur, AVG. Ep. 25, 2;
quas debuit abluere, *easdem* uobis cogatur inferre, CASS. Var. 8, 29, '(so that the filth) which she should have washed from herself, she should not be forced to make it flow back towards you'.

2.4 *Ille*

§145 **2.4.1** *Ille* is used with the ordinary force of a personal pronoun of the third person:

melius enim erat *illis* (= eis) non cognoscere uiam iustitiae, VVLG. 2 Petr. 2, 21 (αὐτοῖς).

§146 **2.4.2** *Ille...ille*, in place of *hic...ille*, with an indefinite meaning:

in illo uel illo templo, AVG. Ciu. 1, 2, 'in such and such a temple'; cf. Parm. 2, 8, 18.

In liturgical and legal formulas, *ille* means 'so-and-so', and it stands where the proper noun will be found.

§147 **2.4.3** Pleonastic use:

utinam *ille* mentitus sit, HIER. Ep. 117, 8;

qui per legem *illi* mundabantur, Tract. (Morin, Anec. III, 2, p. 422, 14) (cf. §132 and §185).

§148 **2.4.4** It can replace a reflexive pronoun:

uerentur ne omnis *illorum* religio inanis sit, LACT. Inst. 2, 2, 9 'their own religion';

ne conferrent cum *illo* (= secum), AVG. C. Cresc. 1, 14, 17;

Martinianus nesciens quid de *illo* (= de se) decreuerat Deus, VICT.-VIT. 1, 31 (analogous examples will be seen later in the sections on reflexive pronouns [§172-§176]).

§149 **2.4.5** It is found in place of *ipse*:

disciplina *medici* exaltabit caput illius, VVLG. Eccli. 38, 3.

§150 **2.4.6** In place of *hic*, to indicate what follows:

illud etiam *quod* crebras inter eos seditiones exagitat, CASS. Var. 1, 32.

§151 **2.4.7** Moreover, it serves as the antecedent to *qui* more often than in Classical Latin:

quasi *illis* minor sit *qui*...ad Dominum glorioso itinere uenerunt, CYPR. Ep. 10.

§152 **2.4.8** Sometimes it is equivalent to the Greek article:

sed *populus ille* memoratae urbis, PASS. VII MON. 9;

exiit ergo Petrus et *ille alius* discipulus, VVLG. Io. 20, 3;

Iudas non *ille Iscariotes*, Io. 14, 22;

illis mendacium *prophetantibus* sacerdotes manibus applauserunt, HIER. Ier. 2, 5, 30;

cf. ITAL. Dan. 9, 5, ap. PS.-CYPR. Pasch. comp. 13.

2.5 *Inde*

§153 Even in Classical Latin this adverb means 'from that, from there.' But this use is extended, and the word tends to have the same meaning as the

French personal pronoun *en* [which can mean 'from that, about that, some,' or 'any']:

de hac re iudicauerunt... *inde* iudicauerunt, AVG. C. Cresc. 4, 7, 9;
mori *inde*, Bapt. 1, 8, 11, 'to die from it';
inde se iactant, Post gest. Don. 17, 21, 'they boasted about that';
te paenitet *inde*, COMM. Instr. 1, 25, 7;

even in speaking about persons:

inde aliquos, CYPR. Eccl. un. 20, 'some people from among them';
potestas *inde* tribuitur, Dom. orat. 25, 'the power comes from him (from God)';
inde est imperator, *unde*..., TERT. Apol. 30, 'he is emperor through the One by whom (he has been created)'.

2.6 *Ipse*

§154 **2.6.1** It is generally used in place of *idem* (earlier in *Suetonius*):

ex ipso ore procedit benedictio et maledictio, VVLG. Iac. 3, 10 (ἐκ τοῦ αὐτοῦ);
id ipsum corpus, TERT. Apol. 48, 'the same body' (for *idipsum*, see *is*);
nec uigore et *robore ipso* ualere *quo* ante praeualebat, CYPR. Ad Demetr. 3;
nunc *ipsi* describuntur *qui* et ante descripti sunt, HIER. Did. spir. 47.

§155 **2.6.2** In place of the reflexive pronoun (earlier in Seneca and Quintus Curtius):

ait Saluator ostendens...aliud *ipsius* bonitate...concedendum, FILASTR. 82, 4;
ut optent se legibus teneri, quae *ab ipsis* sciuntur potuisse constitui, CASS. Var. 6, 4, 2,... 'from laws that one knows well have been able to establish themselves'.

§156 In imitation of the Greek, it gives the reflexive meaning to some pronouns of the first and second person:

tu *de te ipso* testimonium perhibes, VVLG. Io. 8, 13 (περὶ σεαυτοῦ);

or reinforces the meaning of a possessive:

tuam ipsius animam, ITAL. ap. AMBR. Luc. 2, 60.

§157 **2.6.3** It is sometimes equivalent to the Greek article:

ipsi Dauid (title of several psalms); cf. VVLG. 3 Esdr. 8, 15; ITAL. Is. 53, 9, ap. CYPR. Test. 2, 15; RVF. Interp. Ios. 9, 6.

§158 **2.6.4** Finally, it is used with a demonstrative meaning, or to emphasize:

ab ipsis in ueritate...celebrantur qui *ipsorum* martyrum exempla sequuntur, PS.-AVG. Serm. 225, 1, 'those truly observe the feasts of the martyrs who follow their examples themselves';
neque enim qui generantur per Adam, *idem ipsi omnes* per Christum regenerantur, Peccat. Merit. 1, 15, 19;

or with an emphatic meaning:

Deus, *ipse Deominus, ipse* fecit nos, VVLG. Ps. 99, 3;
ipse est enim de quo prophetice scriptum est, LEO-M. Serm. 3, 1;

or simply to replace *is*:

Ioannes testimonium perhibet *de ipso*, VVLG. Io. 1, 15;
quod *ante ipsum* nihil sit genitum, LACT. Inst. 1, 5, 4;
ad *ipsius* gloriam, CYPR. Ep. 10;
tu *ipsius* dominaberis, FILASTR. 131.

2.7 *Is*

§159 **2.7.1** It is sometimes found in place of the reflexive:

coepit *Iesus* ostendere discipulis suis quia oporteret *eum* ire Hierosolymam, VVLG. Mat. 16, 21; cf. HIER. Mat. 13, 36;
admonuit ut ei (= sibi) rescriberet, AVG. Coll. Don. 1, 3.

§§The pronoun refers to two different persons in the following statement:

solum eum (Deum) adorare eos (homines) debere, FILASTR. 15, 1.

§160 **2.7.2** Contrary to classical usage, the genitives *eius, eorum, earum,* can replace the possessive reflexive *suus*:

orabat Dominum...ut dirigeret uiam *eius*, VVLG. Iudith 12, 8;
quot ne *eorum* differretur interitus et rogauerunt, CYPR. Laps. 8, 'how many even asked that their death not be delayed (to themselves)'.

§161 **2.7.3** Emphatic use, in place of *ille*:

Deum etiam uerum, omnipotentem et *eum* audet angelum dicere, FILASTR. 32, 4;
et erit requies *eius* honor, HIER. Ep. 46, 5 (Is. 11).

§162 **2.7.4** In place of ille:

in psalmo *eo*, FILASTR. 50, 7, 'in the psalm in question'.

§163 **2.7.5** *Idipsum* or *id ipsum* (τὸ αὐτό) means 'the same thing' (TERT., CYPR., HIER., et al.) The different meanings of *in idipsum* will be found in the dictionary.

§§The use as an adjective is more rare and pertains to the literature of translation:

id ipsum deuerticulum, RVF. Greg. interp. 151, 3;
cf. id ipsut, HIPP. Trad. p. 59.

2.8 *Iste*

In the classical period, it has a pejorative connotation or it refers to the second person. In the postclassical period, it replaces any demonstrative pronoun.

§164 **2.8.1** Meaning of *hic*:

istas litteras nostras, AVG. Doct. chr. 4, 3;
isto tempore, Vnic. bapt. 7, 12, 'in our time';
in saeculo *isto*, CYPR. Ep. 73, 19;
mundum *istum*, FILASTR. 31, 2;
de saeculi *istius* somno, AMBR. Ep. 2, 22 (in these last three examples, one can also allow a pejorative connotation);
istae (= meae) quoque litterae testes sunt, HIER. Ep. 14, 1;
sed credimus iam *ista* sufficere, CASS. Var. 6, 19, 7 (one has just spoken of it).

It is opposed to *ille*:

ille annus...*iste* annus ('in which we are'), AMBR. Ep. 18, 23;
ille namque amor ex miseria est, *iste* ex misericordia, AVG. Catech. 4, 7 (the opposition *iste...ille* 'this one...that one' is very frequent in this writer, who also uses the traditional *hic...ille*);
cf. HIER. Ep. 108, 31.

§165 **2.8.2** Meaning of *is*:

iste qui...orbem circuit, AMBR. Ep. 46, 2; 51, 7;
cf. HIER. Ep. 54, 6.

§166 **2.8.3** Meaning of *ille*:

ab *isto* certamine, sed in hoc..., AMBR. Ep. 20, 15;
est enim conuentus *iste* nimia celebritate festiuus, CASS. Var. 8, 33;
post ista, PASS. RVF. p. 444, 'after that'.

3 Personal Pronouns

§167 **3.1** In the Vulgate, the personal pronoun is sometimes replaced by a noun like *anima, facies, nomen, manus, oculus, etc.*:

sollemnitates uestras odiuit anima mea, VVLG. Is. 1, 14;
facies mea praecedet te, Ex. 33, 14, 'I will go before you in person';

quod si pauper est, et not potest manus eius inuenire..., Leu. 14, 21;
pauca nomina (= paucos), Apoc. 3,4;
cf. nolite quicquam horum meis operibus (= mihi) applicare, EVGIPP. Vit. Seu. 14, 3, 'do not impute to me any of these miracles'.

One will see later the formulas used in the 'plural of majesty' and the 'polite plural'; and we have indicated in the section on stylistics [§16] the epistolary or homiletic formulas in which the abstract word is substituted for a personal pronoun.

§168 **3.2** The pronouns *ego* and *tu* are reinforced by *ipse*, in some cases where Classical Latin would use forms such as *egomet, mihimet, tumet*:

meipsum, VVLG. Tob. 9, 2;
meipso, Io. 8, 28;
memetipso, Ier. 22, 5;
nosipsi, 2 Esdr. 4, 21;
nosmetipsos, 2 Cor. 4, 5; etc.

§169 **3.3** We have already pointed out (§80 and §81) the use of the genitive of the personal pronoun in place of the possessive; here are other examples:

mei membra, CYPR. Laps. 4;
mei causa, ITAL. Mat. 10, 18, ap. TERT. Scorp. 9, 'on account of me' (Classical Latin *mea causa*, for *me*);
consiliator *tui*, LEPTOG. 23, 16;
ad exordium *sui*, SALV. Gub. 6, 34 (= suum exordium);
pro inpuritate et obscaenitate *sui*, RVF. Hist. eccl. 2, p. 137, 20, 'because of their own impurity and filthiness';
praesentiam *sui* abnegans, ibid. 10, p. 991, 7 (ἑαυτοῦ).

§170 **3.4** The reflexive can be used pleonastically (ethical dative; cf. *sedete uobis,* §99, at the end).

gaudebat *sibi*, HIER. Tr. in psal. 15, p. 22, 7 (these lectures of Jerome are written in a very familiar style; cf. mihi gaudeo, CIC. Fam. 6,15; gaudebat sibi, SEN., Clem.);
sibi...periit, FVLG. p. 169, 14;
qui...sedit *sibi* foris, BEN. Reg. 43;
ut epistulas ipsas...acciperem *mihi* ab ipso sancto, PEREG. 19, 19.

4 Polite Plural

§171 An emperor, a pope, and a bishop, when addressing their subordinates, used the plural of majesty:

iubemus dilectioni tuae, GREG.-M. Ep. 1, 15.

By analogy, they came to use, when addressing others, the 'polite plural' *uos* and more often the possessive *uester.* Some also give the following explanation: from the time of Diocletian, the power of the empire was divided and seemed to be incarnate in several people; and the practice of addressing that power in the plural survived, even when one was addressing only one emperor:

senatus amplissimus semperque *uester*, SYMM. Ep. 10, 1 (to Valentinian II).

Be that as it may, this usage never became general, even in the Middle Ages.

sub *uestrae* imperio clementiae, *uobis* imperantibus, BONIF. I Ep. 7 (to Honorius);

et *te* dominum meum...scriptis *uestris* alii impertiuntur, MAMERT. Ep. 1, p. 198, 11, '...receive your writings (to Sidonius);

pia serenitatis *uestrae* protectio, GREG.-M. Ep. 6, 16 (to the emperor);

quanquam...filio paterna *uos* pietate nouerimus impendere, Ep. 10, 47, 'although I know that you show your paternal sollicitude for the son' (to John, the bishop of Syracuse);

quem (librum) non *uestrae* specialiter instituo potestati...sed generaliter his conscripsi, quos ministeriis *tuis* astantes haec conuenit legere, MART.-BRAC. Form. praef. (to Miro, king of Galicia).

Hence, the plural is seen, in several examples, to alternate with the singular.

5 Reflexives and Possessives

5.1 The classical rules fall into disuse; one finds then

§172 **5.1.1** *Suus,* in place of *eius* and *eorum,*

5.1.1.1 in main clauses, where the possessor is not the subject:

illuc quoque *sua* fama peruenerat, HIER. Vit. Hil. 34;

solus pater defensionem *suam* (fratris accusati) opponere..., Ep. 125, 13;

cf. AVG. Emer. 9; CYPR. Ep. 58, 4; VICT.-VIT. 3, 26; etc.

In certain cases, one might suppose that it is a matter of the classical exception, when *suus* means 'one's own' [AG 301d]; but the position of the words is not the same:

ecclesiae catholicae corpus *suum* scindere nituntur, CYPR. Ep. 44, 3.

§173 **5.1.1.2** more often in subordinate clauses, when the possessor is not the subject of the main clause:

numquid uoluit (Ioannes) apud se remanere discipulos suos? AVG. Tr. eu. Io. 7, 8, 'Did John want to keep his disciples close to him?' (disciples of Jesus).

§174 **5.1.2** The reflexive pronoun *sui, sibi, se,* in place of the corresponding cases of *is, ea, id,* when it in no way refers to the subject:

se (= eos) profecturos...Renatus clamauerit, AMBR. Ep. 5, 20;
(Petrus) repente audit a Domino oportere *se* (= eum, sc. Dominum) ire Hierosolymam, HIER. Mat. 3, 16, 22;
cum eis qui *secum* (= eum eo) erant, AVG. Parm. 2, 15, 34;
factus est...Cornelius episcopus...cum nemo ante *se* factus esset, CYPR. Ep. 55, 8 (in Classical Latin, this clause could have the underlying meaning: 'although he knew that no one before him...').

The pronoun replaces even a noun referring to a thing:

opuscula mea quae non *sui* merito sed tua bonitate desiderare te dicis. HIER. Ep. 72, 5;
iuxta se (= eam), THEOD. Sit. 7.

§175 **5.1.3** *Eum* in place of *se*:

exinde *coepit Iesus ostendere* discipulis suis, quia oporteret *eum* ire Hierosolymam, VVLG. Mat. 16, 21 (see other examples under the use of *is*).

§176 **5.1.4** *Eius* and *eorum* in place of *suus* (see under the use of *is*).

5.2 The possessive *suus* is sometimes

§177 **5.2.1** reinforced by *ipse* (earlier in *Livy*)

suis ipsi tormentis occupati, LACT. Inst. 6, 4, 20;

or by *sibi* (PL., APVL.):

de *suo sibi* fecit, TERT. Marc. 2, 3;
sua sibi opera praetulerunt, LACT. Inst. 2, 5, 6 (compare the pleonastic use of the reflexive pointed out above, see §170).

§178 **5.2.2** replaced by *proprius* (TREB., SPART., AMM.):

nec *propria* eius adsumptio, sed caelestis uocatio, AMBR. Ep. 64, 48; cf. propriae uirtutis, Ep. 19, 29;
ad propria reuerti, remeare, AVG. C. Cresc. 3, 43, 47; Coll. Don. 1, 14, 'to return to one's home'.

Notice that *proprius* can also replace *tuus, noster, etc.*:

propriis textuisti litteris, AMBR. Ep. 56, 6;
propriae salutis (= tuae), CASS. Var. 1, 2;
propria...sponte, Var. 4, 20, 'of our own will'.

5.3 Other remarks concerning the personal and reflexive pronouns:

§179 **5.3.1** As in the first and second persons, the possessive is often replaced by the genitive of the reflexive pronoun:

propter nobilitatem *sui* (= suam), CASS. Var. praef. 18;
ad tutelam *sui*, LACT. Opif. 2, 4, 'for its defense' (objective genitive);
sui proponit exemplum HIER. Ep. 48, 13, 'his example' (subjective genitive).

§180 **5.3.2** Inversely, one finds possessives in some cases where Classical Latin used the personal pronoun:

uota *tua* (= erga te), VVLG. Ps. 55, 12, 'the prayers that I have offered up to you';
improperiorum *tuorum*, Ps. 73, 23, 'the insults that one has addressed to you';
hoc facite in *meam* commemorationem, Luc. 22, 19.

6 Reciprocity

It is expressed not only by *inter se, alius alium*, and *alter alterum*, as in Classical Latin, but more often

§181 **6.1** by *alteruter*, 'mutual, reciprocal':

(adjective) *alterutro* ardore, AVG. Ep. 211, 10;
alterutra oppositio, TERT. Pud. 2;
simus orationibus nostris *alterutri* adiutores, CYPR. Ep. 77, 3;
(pronoun) osculari se *alterutrum*, VVLG. 1 Reg. 20, 41;
dicentes ad *alterutrum*, Judith 5, 26;
idipsum sapere in *alterutrum*, Rom 15, 5, 'to have the same feelings for each other';
pro *alterutro* mori parati, TERT. Apol. 39;
dixerunt ad *alterutrum*, HIER. Ep. 18, 6;
coniuges qui ab *alterutro* separati sunt, AVG. Nupt. et conc. 1, 10, 11.

Alterutrum or *alterutro* is used also adverbially, with the meaning 'mutually, reciprocally': TERT. Vx. 2, 8; HIER. Gal. 3, 6, 5; etc.

§182 **6.2** by the adverb *invicem* (earlier in PLIN.-I., TAC., QUINT.)

a. either alone:

suscipite *inuicem*, VVLG. Rom. 15, 7;
crimina inuicem donare, AVG. C. Gaud. 1, 37, 47;

b. or with another pronoun:

inuicem uos ametis, HIER. Ep. 7, 1;
nisi se inuicem fratres mutua tolerantia foueant, CYPR. Bon. pat. 15;
sibimet inuicem, AVG. Conf. 6, 10; 8, 2;

c. even with a preposition:

separari ab inuicem, CYPR. Ad Demetr. 19;
ab se inuicem separare, Ep. 4, 4;

aduersus inuicem, ITAL. 1 Cor. 6, 7, ap. CYPR. Test. 3, 44; PS.-CYPR. Sing. 19, 'one against the other';
ad inuicem, 'one towards the other': PS.-CYPR. Sing. 19; HIER. Is. 3, 6, 2; VVLG. Ex. 16, 16; Io. 13, 35;
in inuicem, Rom. 1, 27; 1 Thess. 3, 12;
pro inuicem, 1 Cor. 12, 25; AVG. Conf. 4, 6;
post inuicem, Conf. 7, 6, 'one after the other'.

§183 **6.3** by the simple reflexive:
adfectione concordes, fideliter *sibi* unianimitatis nexibus *cohaerentes*, CYPR. Eccl. un. 2, 4;
ut *se* pares animi solent semper *eligere*, CASS. Var. 1, 4.

§§184 **6.4** Isolated example:
inter se, MINVC. 18, 1 (= inter nos).

7 Relative Pronoun

§185 **7.1** The use of the redundant demonstrative in a relative clause (rare archaism, APVL., AMM., VOP.):
qui per legem *illi* mundabantur, fasciculo hysopi aspergebantur, HIER. Comm. psal. 50 (Morin, Anec. III, 2, p. 422, 14);
pereat dies *in quo* natus sum *in* eo, VVLG. Iob 3, 3 (ἐν ᾗ ἐγεννήθην ἐν αὐτῇ);
cuius non sum dignus soluere corrigiam calceamentorum *eius*, Luc. 3, 16 (οὗ...αὐτοῦ);
beatus uir *cuius* est nomen Domini spes *eius*, Ps. 39, 5.

In the following example, the pleonastic use of two demonstratives serves an expressive purpose:
quos cum *ipsos* iusserit Deus...opibus renuntiare, *illi* eas cupiunt possidere, SALV. Eccl. 2, 22, 'these people, whom God has especially commanded to renounce wealth, are those who want to possess it'.

§186 **7.2** One finds some examples of the attraction of the relative as in Greek (very rare in Classical Latin):
uita *in hac, qua* (= quam) nunc ego dego, senili, P.-PELL. Euch. 598;
comprehenduntur *consiliis quibus* cogitant, VVLG. Ps. 9, 23;
quibus inde conceperat *uiribus*, TERT. Val. 16, 'with the forces which he had gathered from there (in Classical Latin when the antecedent appears with the relative, it is governed by the verb of that relative: quas uires inde conceperat, iis...).

The antecedent itself can take the case of the relative (a rare attraction in Classical Latin, frequent in Late Latin):

sermonem, quem audistis, non *est* meus, VVLG. Io. 14, 24 (sermo in many of the mss., the attraction does not appear in the Greek text);
me miserum, quem uides, de Roma *sum*, VIT. PATR. 5, 10, 76;
panem, quem angelorum appellat, manna *est*, PS.-AVG. Qu. test. 20, 1;
fabricam, quam uides, ecclesia *est*, PEREG. 13, 4;
titulus, qui ad caput Domini positus erat, *uidi*, ANTON. Itin. 20.

§187 **7.3** The relative is sometimes equivalent to a Greek article:
docebat uerissime *quae* iuxta Iesum, ITAL. Act. 18, 25, ap. AVG. C. Cresc. 1, 11, 14 (τὰ περὶ τοῦ 'Ιησοῦ);
correptio haec *quae multis*, ITAL. 2 Cor. 2, 6, ap. AVG. Parm. 3, 2, 14 (ἡ ὑπὸ τῶν πλειόνων) (quae fit a pluribus, VVLG.).
§§The scholastics will translate the τὸ τί ἦν εἶναι of Aristotle by *quod quid erat esse* 'the fact of being what it was, the essence'.

§188 **7.4** As in Greek, the demonstrative, in a second relative, can replace the relative pronoun (rare in Cicero):
beatus uir *cui* non imputabit Dominus peccatum, nec est in spiritu *eius* dolus, VVLG. Ps. 31, 2.

§189 **7.5** The neuter relative *quod* is found after an expression of time:
tertia dies est *quod*, VVLG. Luc. 24, 21, 'it is the third day that....'
The study of subordinate clauses will provide us with an opportunity to record the growth of expressions with *quod.*

§190 **7.6** Suppression of the correlative [cp. AG 152] after a preposition (it is, again, a Hellenism):
secundum quod dictum est, VVLG. Luc. 2, 24;
de omnibus quibus accusor, Act. 26, 2 (περὶ πάντων ὧν ἐγκαλοῦμαι);
retribuat tibi bona pro quibus (καθῶς) fecisti, ITAL. 1 Reg. 24, 20, ap. LVCIF. Athan. 1, 15, 'for that which you have done' (notice also the attraction);
crudele est ut, de quo habes, non des, PS.-AVG. Serm. 310, 2.

§191 **7.7** Certain relative adverbs play the role of a pronoun:
1. *Vbi* is used in this way earlier in Classical Latin, but with more freedom later:
omnicreantis Dei *ubi* (= in quo) amoris fructuosissimus finis est, AVG. Catech. 12, 17.
2. The same is true for *unde*:

de baptismo sanguinis *unde* te iactas, AVG. C. littl. Petil. 2, 23, 58, 'of which you boast';
gaude *unde ille* coactus est flere, PS.-CYPR. (Hart. app. p. 277), 'rejoice at that which ought to make him weep'.

A conjunctive relative pronoun followed by the subjunctive is equivalent to *ut inde*:

statim diuinae censurae maiestate percussus est, unde regrediens impetu ac morsu leonis necaretur, CYPR. Ep. 59, 6, 'so that he had to die as he was coming back from it....'

See the syntax of subordinate relative clauses.

8 Interrogatives

§192 **8.1** As in Greek, a question can focus on two words in the same clause:

ut ostenderet *quid cui* debeat esse subiectum, TERT. Mart. 4, 'who ought to be obedient and to whom';
bellando *quis quem* ualebat expellere, IORD. Get. 152, 'while fighting about who can expel the other';
quis quid diceret, VICT.-VIT. 3, 19.

§§One even finds two relatives, which appear to be an isolated example: petierunt...unusquisque monasteria sua, *qui ubi* habebat, PEREG. 20, 7, 'they returned to their hermitages, each one to where his was'.

§193 **8.2** One encounters *quis* in place of *uter* when it is a question of two persons or of two things:

quis ex duobus fecit uoluntatem patris? VVLG. Mat. 21, 31;
cui de duobus adsistimus, CYPR. Ep. 55, 19;
cf. TERT. An. 13; SALV. Gub. 3, 26.

§194 **8.3** *qui* for the adjective *uter*: TERT. Virg. uel. 2; Herm. 25.

§195 **8.4** *qui* for *qualis*:

memorare *quae* mea substantia, VVLG. Ps. 88, 48 (pejorative sense = qualis, quam infirma).

§196 **8.5** *qui* for *quis*;

TERT. Scorp. 11; Spect. 15; SEDVL. Carm. pasch. 1, 221.

§197 **8.6** *quanti* for *quot* or *quam multi*:

quantae uirgines, HIER, Ep. 64, 22;
quanti monachorum suas animas perdiderunt, Ep. 64, 4;

quanta iacula, CYPR. Bon. pat. 18.

9 Correlatives

§198 We point out only the frequent use of *tanti...quanti*, with the meaning of *tot...quot*:

tantae urbes (nunc exstant) quantae non casae quondam, TERT. An. 30, 'more cities today than formerly houses';
quantis potuit militibus, LACT. Mort. 45, 7, 'with as many soldiers as he could'.

10 Indefinites

§199 The use of the indefinites calls for numerous comments, but they are more a concern of the dictionary.

Keep in mind principally:

toti, with the meaning of *omnes;*
diuersus, with the meaning of an indefinite (*quidam*);
quisque, with the meaning of *quisquis*;
quisquis and *quicumque*, used as simple indefinites, whereas *quiuis* and *quilibet* move to the ranks of indefinite relatives.

Some nouns, such as *facies* and *homo*, can acquire the meaning of simple indefinites.

5 Agreement

§§200 **1.** Verb or predicate in the singular when the subject is a neuter plural (a Hellenism), especially with *omnia, haec, reliqua, etc.*:

in parabolis *omnia dicitur*, ITAL. Marc. 4, 11 (cod. Cant.);
quae interpretati sumus de ecclesia *potest* intelligi, HIER. (Morin, Études I, p. 250) (familiar lectures);
reliqua...impleatur, BEN. Reg. 18;
cf. COMM. Instr. 1, 34, 18; GREG.-T. Mart. 4, 45; PEREG. 36, 4.

§§201 **2.** In the Psalms of the Vulgate, a neuter pronoun is replaced by a feminine (a Hebraism):

unam petii a Domino, Ps. 26, 4, 'only one thing';
haec facta est mihi, Ps. 118, 56, 'this happened to me';
cf. Mich. 4, 6 (unless one understands *gens*).

§§202 **3.** The relative in the neuter can be found after the antecedent *res*:

de rubus quae (= quas) in oculis habemus, CAES.-AREL. (Moris p. 256, 27).

§203 **4.** Agreement according to the meaning:

si *quis* non intelligit...intue*antur*, AVG. Bapt. 1, 4, 5;
personae cognoscerent se esse sub*actos*, VICT.-VIT. 3, 9.

The verb with a collective subject in the singular tends to take the plural form more freely than in Classical Latin:

consol*amini*, popule meus, VVLG. Is. 40, 1;
haeresis, quae...non desine*bant*, FILASTR. 27, 1;
pars Donati qui...occid*unt*, AVG. C. Guad. 1, 27, 31.

Notice this first person plural:

serenitas nostra...corroboramus, CASS. Var. 8, 25;

and this participle in the plural is governed by a subject in the singular;

ut aestimantes...prudentia uestra reponat, Var. 5, 43.

§204 **5.** In the following example, the same word is used as object and as subject:

quae Graeci περίδειπνα *uocant* et a nostris uulgo *appellantur* parentalia, HIER. Ier. (CSEL. 59, p. 197, 8).

§205 **6.** The direct or indirect object [*complément d'objet*] can be a partitive phrase formed mainly with the preposition *de*:

tollent de cineribus, VVLG. Num. 19, 17, 'they will take some ashes' (see other examples under the preposition *de* in the dictionary);
ex omni ligno paradisi comede, Gen. 2, 16.

These phrases can be the subject of a passive verb:

et dabitur ei *de auro* Arabiae, Ps. 71, 15.

The following seem to be Hebraisms:

erant *ex Pharisaeis*, Io. 1, 24, 'they were Pharisees';
quem appretiauerunt *a filiis Israhel*, Mat. 27, 9, 'such a one whom the sons of Israel esteemed'.

§206 **7.** Appositive replaced by a modifier of a noun [*complément du nom*], according to the pattern of *oppidum Stridonis*; see the sections on the genitive [esp. §91].

§§207 **8.** The complement of the direct object [*l'attribut du complément d'objet*, in English usually called the objective complement] can be in the nominative with the word *nomen*:

iam *corona nomen* habebat, PS.-AVG. Serm. 211, 1, 'was called crown' (Saint Stephen).
(pleonasm) uocabis *nomen eius Iesus*, VVLG. Mat. 1, 21 (καλέσεις τὸ ὄνομα αὐτοῦ 'Ιησοῦν) cf. Is. 9, 6.
(without *nomen*) 'dendros alethia', quod nos dicimus 'arbor ueritatis', PEREG. 9, 4;
in septimana paschale, quam hic appellant *septimana* maior, ibid. 30, 1

§208 **9.** Some instances of lack of agreement may be slips by copyists:

similes pueris sedentibus et ad inuicem dicentes (= dicentibus), ITAL. Luc. 7, 32;
sermonem *quod*, Io. 15, 3, ap. PS.-AVG. C. Fulg. Don. 5;
eumdem oleum, ibid. 15;
illi *renuncians* (= renuntianti) rescissa sit omnis res, PS.-CYPR. Spect. 4;
negotium perambulan*tem*, ARN.-I. Ad. Greg. 17;
uultum Dei *quod*..., HIER. Tr. I in psal. p. 267, 25;
maio*rem* opprobrium, VICT.-VIT. 1, 44.

6 Syntax of the Verb

1 General remarks

One will find in the dictionary:

§209 **1.1** Transitive verbs used absolutely, such as *adorare, apponere* 'to give gifts', *annuntiare, praestare* 'to do a service', *trahere* 'to continue', *uehere* 'to travel', *etc.*;

§210 **1.2** Transitive verbs used intransitively, such as *inclinare*; or as reflexive verbs such as *reficere* for *se reficere*; or in place of the passive, such as *intimat* for *intimatur*;

§211 **1.3** Intransitive verbs used as transitives, such as *exultare* and *pluere*;

§212 **1.4** Deponent verbs used in the active form, such as *lamentare* and *radicare*;

§213 **1.5** Active verbs used in the deponent form, such as *certari, lacrymari* and *malignari*;

§214 **1.6** Deponent verbs used in the passive voice, such as *consolari, uesci, admirari,* and *hortari*;

§215 **1.7** Impersonal verbs used personally, such as *decere, oportere, paenitere, etc.*

2 Use of Tenses

2.1 Tenses in the translation of the Vulgate

In the Psalms and in the books of the Old Testament that have a prophetic character, the interpretation of the tenses of Hebrew has often been warped by the Greek translation of the Septuagint, a warp which has been transmitted into the Latin translations. Hebrew has only two tenses, which express two aspects, the perfect and the imperfect; but either can just as easily indicate the present, the past, or the future. The translation of the Septuagint has taken the perfect as a past, and the imperfect as a future; hence, in the Vulgate, the past tenses have taken the place

§216 **2.1.1** of a present:

sepulchrum patens *est* guttur eorum, linguis suis dolose *agebant* (ἐδολιοῦσαν, SEPT.), Ps. 5, 11, 'with their language, they weave deceits';

§§cf. ego baptizo in aqua: medius autem *stetit*, quem uos nescitis, Io. 1, 26, 'but he is already in the midst of you' (this can be a perfect brought from the Greek στήκει, a present tense formed on ἕστηκα; moreover, the Latin perfect often has by itself the meaning of an accomplished present).

§217 **2.1.2** of a future:

notas mihi *fecisti* (ἐγνώρισας, SEPT.) uias uitae, *adimplebis* me laetitia cum uultu tuo, Ps. 15, 11, 'you will teach me the ways of life';

uiuificabis me et super iram inimicorum meorum *extendisti* (ἐξέτεινας, SEPT.) manum tuam, Ps. 13, 7;

§218 **2.1.3** just as a future can have the meaning of a present:

tu *benedices* (εὐλογήσεις, SEPT.) iusto, Domine, ut scuto bonae uoluntatis tuae *coronasti* nos, Ps. 5, 13, 'you bless the just...';

quoniam *uidebo* (ὄψομαι, SEPT.), Ps. 8, 3, 'when I consider'.

§§Note: In St. Jerome's translation, a perfect corresponds to a future of the Septuagint:

uocaui, Is. 45, 4 (καλέσω).

2.2 Periphrastic forms

2.2.1 With *habere*:

§219 **2.2.1.1** *Habere* with the passive participle is often equivalent to a perfect; it is the construction which belongs to the origins of the French *passé composé*:

cuius etiam capillos tu, Domine, numeratos habes, AVG. Conf. 4, 14, 'whose hairs you have counted';

ea uerba quae ex Hebraeo in Latinum non habemus expressa, HIER. Ep. 26, 1, 'that we have not translated'.

The dictionary will provide other examples under the words *subiectus, subditus, repositus, etc*. In these sentences, as in the analogous constructions that are found earlier in Cicero, one can always say that it is a matter of expressing an accomplished present: 'God has them present in his memory' or 'our translation is now presenting this peculiarity'. But in the following example, the idea of the past is dominant:

metuo enim ne ibi uos *habeam fatigatos*, AVG. Serm. 37, 17, 'I fear having wearied you there (in that report), (undoubtedly, 'I have before me some tired listeners', but especially 'I tired you a short while ago').

§220 **2.2.1.2** *Haberem* with the past participle indicates our pluperfect:

si Dominum *iratum haberes*, AVG. Serm 211, 2, 'if you were to have angered, if you had angered the Lord' (supposition in the past, rather than unreal of the past [= contrary-to-fact of the past; see GL 597 and AG 514]).

§221 **2.2.1.3** *Habere*, followed by the infinitive of a verb of assertion with the meaning of 'I can, I have to (say)'. This use developed from the second century on in the literature of translation, and St. Jerome in turn has increased the number of these constructions:

multa *habui* tibi *scribere*, VVLG. Io. 3 Ep. 1, 13 (εἶχον γράψαο).

Writers have used the same construction with other verbs.[26]

non *habebant saluari*, IREN. 3, 20, 3, 'they could not be saved'.

Then there is the idea of obligation which becomes the most important:

habebat inquiri ut occideretur, IREN. 4, 20, 12, 'one was obliged to look (had to look) for him to kill him'.

excludi ac *respui* magis *habebat*, TERT. An. 32;

si natus *credi habebat*, Adu. Marc. 3, 11, 'if one was obliged to believe (had to believe) that He was born';

nasci habebat, Virg. uel. 6, 'had to be born';

habet nubere, Monog. 7:

unum *habet esse* baptisma, CYPR. Sent. 73;

trinitas quae *manifestari habebat*, Dom. orat. 34.

From the idea of necessity, one passes to the idea of the future, of the immediate future, especially with the passive infinitive:

---

[26] On the other hand, in the following examples:

non habent retribuere tibi, VVLG. Luc. 14, 14;

ego cibum habeo manducare, Io. 4, 32 (ἔχω φαψεῖν),

habeo, followed by the infinitive preserves its earliest meaning: 'they cannot, that is to say, they do not have the wherewithal to pay you'.

See the infinitive of purpose in the chapter on the infinitive.

quod a fratribus suis laudari et adorari haberet, CYPR. Ep. 63, 6, 'because he had to be later, because he would be praised and honored by his brothers';

ad gloriam quae in nos *habeat reuelari*, ITAL. Rom. ap. TERT. Scorp. 13, 'which would be (μέλλουσα) revealed to us';

audiri habebant, PASS. BON. ET MAX. (Ruin.), 'they were going to be understood';

qui flagellari et occidi haberent, IREN. 3, 18, 5,'those who would be whipped or killed'.

The present *habeo* and the imperfect *habebam* followed by the infinitive belong to the origins of our French future and conditional. In the following examples, the idea of the future (or of the future in the past, with *habebam*), appears at least as much as the idea of obligation:

incipere habebat, AMBR. Hex. 1, 9;

et sic nihil *habes inuenire* in manibus tuis, AVG.Serm. 39, 5;

qui nasci habent, HIER. In Eccl. 1, c. 1072, 'those who will be born, who ought to be born'.

§§222 **2.2.2** *Debeo*, followed by the infinitive, expresses sometimes the idea of the future:

postulauit ut horologium...ei *transmittere debeamus*, CASS. Var. 1, 45 (one can also consider this construction as pleonastic = transmitteremus, like the constructions of the following paragraph:)

se *relaxari debuisse* precibus speranti, GREG.-M. Ep. (Ew. I, p. 442, 25), 'hoping that his prayers would have caused him to be released';

ut...inconsignati non *debeant remanere*, ibid. II, p. 262, 14, 'so that they do not remain without being confirmed'.

§223 **2.2.3** Periphrastic forms are found with verbs other than *debeo*, and these verbs do not seem to have a full meaning:

nisi recta *uidere coeperint*, HIER. Ier. 1, 3, 2 (= uiderint);

qua ratione de tam longo itinere huc *pergere demonstraris*, VICT.-VIT. 2, 30 (= pergis), 'why does one see you come...'(cf. with *coepisse, dignari, uelle,* ibid. 1, 18; 1, 15; 1, 27);

quibus custodes *uidemur esse* praepositi, GREG.-M.Ep. 4, 35, p. 271, 3;

qui nostrae aulae *uidentur*[27] *excubare*, CASS., Var. 1, 10 (= excubant), 'that one is of service, who are of service to our court';

---

[27] In the following sentences *uideri* alone is the equivalent of *esse*:

ubi munitiones aliquae uidebantur, VICT.-VIT. 1, 9, 'were seen, were';

qui infantulus uidebatur, PASS. VII MON. 12.

quibusdam etiam *nititur uelle* superare, Var. 1, 45 (*nititur uelle* pleonastic form);
nec quidquam *liceat habere*, BEN. Reg. 33 (= habeat);
ut...*referre* gratias...*ualeamus*, GREG.-M. Ep. 9, 13 (= referamus);
poteritis liberari, EUGIPP. Vit. Seu. p. 15, 18 (= liberabimini).

However, *possum* itself can also form some kinds of periphrastic futures (SPART., TREB.):

ratus hunc *succedere posse* mox sibimet, SEDVL. Carm. 2, 79;
posse se mandatis *oboedire*, EVGIPP. Vit. 16, 7, 'that he would obey';

as well as *incipio* (μέλλω) and *volo*:

incipiam te euomere, VVLG. Apoc. 3, 16; cf. CYPR. Dom. orat. 9;
uerba haec quae tibi incipio dicere, HERM. Past. 1, 1, 1; IREN. 1, 13, 3;
uolentes (μέλλοντες) suscipere, Act. 20, 13 (cod. Laud.);
cf. HIER. Ep. 27, 2.

§224 **2.2.4** Examples of pleonastic expressions with verbs meaning 'to say' (biblical style):

clamauerunt dicentes, Mat. 8, 29;
rogabant eum dicentes, Mat. 8, 31;
deprecabatur...dicens, Marc. 5, 23;
locutus est eis Iesus *dicens*, Io. 8, 12; etc.;
docet dicens, LACT. Inst. 4, 4, 4;
adiecit et ait, ibid. 4, 12, 16:
clamans quid nos *admonet* vox *dicens*, BEN. Reg. prol.
(See the chapter on participles).

§225 **2.2.5** *Sum* constructed with a present participle is a Hellenism:

et *erat* plebs *exspectans*, VVLG. Luc. 1, 21(ἦν...προσδοκῶν);
et erunt decidentes, Sap. 4, 19, 'they will fall';
non enim *sumus...adulterantes* uerbum Dei, 2 Cor. 2, 17;
sic uitiis adhaerentibus *obsecundans eram*, CYPR.Ad Don. 4;
non sint contradicentes, HIER. Tit. 2, 9;
paruulos *indigentes esse* Christi liberatoris auxilio, AVG. C. Iul. 1, 6, 23; cf. Conf. 1, 10; 4, 4;
si scientes essent, AMBR. Psal. 43, 58;
qui *erant* in heremo commorantes, CASSIAN. Coll. 10, 2, 3;
sit praeualens, BEN. Reg. 2 (= praeualeat);
quem *sequentes fuerunt* forsitan per passus centum, PEREG. 16, 6;

§§ even when the verb *esse* is understood:

ingressi sumus in sanctam ciuitatem, in qua *adorantes* (fuimus) monumentum Domini, ANTON. Itin. 18;

§§even with the gerundive, which already expresses the future:

in futuro *erunt deputandi*, FILASTR. 150, 9;
supra multa nimis *constituendus eris*, FORT. 5, 2, 56.

One also finds this periphrasis with the future participle, in place of a simple future:

an hoc dicturi sunt? AVG. Parm. 4, 3, 24;
perditurus es animam tuam, VICT.-VIT. 3, 50;
si cenaturi sunt, BEN. Reg. 39.

2.3 Comments on the use of tenses proper[28]

See the chapter on the infinitive and the participle for the use of tenses in those moods.

§226 **2.3.1** As in the colloquial language of the classical period, the present can replace the future:

quando *salutamus* amicos maiores? AVG. Conf. 6, 11, 'when are we going to save our older friends?'
tempus meum prope est: apud te *facio* (ποιῶ) Pascha cum discipulis meis, VVLG. Mat. 26, 18;
scribat amicis suis...et ego *scribo* coepiscopis meis, VICT.-VIT. 2, 44;
horre uitium et principis *mereris* affectum, CASS. Var. 7, 2.

Inversely, one finds the future, in place of the present:

sicut in trigonis et tetragonis puncta sunt, sic et in circulo eius medium puncto *possidebitur*, MAMERT. St. an. 1, 25, 'just as there are points in three- or four-sided figures, so a point will mark the center of a circumference'.

§227 **2.3.2** In the following example, the imperfect of attempted action is more daring than in Classical Latin:

et *uocabant* eum nomine patris eius Zachariam, VVLG. Luc. 1, 59, 'they wanted to call (ἐκαλοῦν)'.

§228 **2.3.3** Future in place of an imperative:

et cum oratis, non eritis sicut hypocritae, VVLG. Mat. 6, 5;
uade et dices, VICT.-VIT. 2, 47 (see below the use of moods).

§229 **2.3.4** Future perfect, in place of the simple future (cf. *uidero*, I shall see, in the letters of Cicero):

quis hoc negauerit? AVG. Ciu. 2, 4, 'who will deny it?'

---

[28] With regard to the use of tenses and moods in a not-so-refined time, it is necessary to keep in mind that it is perhaps a matter of orthographical variants: e.g. *cum aliquis suscipit nomen abbatis*, BEN. Reg. 2 (or *suscepit*?); cf. the endings *-auit, -abit*, each taken for the other in Gregory of Tours.

§230 **2.3.5** Just as the Greek aorist, the perfect[29] can express a habitual action or a general truth (gnomic aorist); it is a postclassical or poetical usage:

sollemnitates uestras *odiuit* anima mea, VVLG. Is. 1, 14, 'I hate' (Classical Latin *odi*);

plerique (= multi)...et usque ad senectutis aetatem uitam *produxere* maculosam, AMBR. Psal. 1, 27.

§231 **2.3.6** Just as the Greek aorist, the perfect can have the meaning of a pluperfect:

et non apparuit, quia *tulit* eum Deus, VVLG. Gen. 5, 24;

cum ipsi receperint quod ore proprio *damnauerunt* (= damnauerant), AVG. Parm. 2, 3, 7.

§232 **2.3.7** In subordinate clauses, the pluperfect of the subjunctive begins to be used with the meaning of an imperfect;

ne cenasset, TERT. Pall. 5, 'in order that he might not dine at all';

si potuissent, ARN. 1, 33 (= si possent, unreal of the present [or contrary-to-fact, see GL 597 and AG 514];

petiit ut reuerti *licuisset*, OPTAT. 1, 26 (= liceret);

sufficere debuerat...ut instauratio peccatorum non *instaurasset* excidium, SALV. Gub. 6, 75 (but here with the underlying meaning of accomplished action: 'it is a thing done, unfortunately';

cum *ignorasset*...ilico iussit, VICT.-VIT. 1, 20.

§233 **2.3.8** The use of the perfect of the subjunctive, in place of a present, to soften an assertion appears only in the period of the Empire (QVINT., PLIN.-I., etc.):

quadam dixerim resurrectione, CYPR. Ep. 39, 5;

ut ita dixerim, SALV. Gub. 5, 58 (Ciceronian language would normally have *ut ita dicam*).

On the other hand, the use of the same tense, with the potential meaning, is not unknown in Classical Latin:

si ergo hoc *dixerint*,...intelligant, AVG. Bapt. 1, 12, 12.

It is a matter of expressing an eventuality accomplished in the future: 'if they would say it, as soon as this would be said by them'; it is analogous to the use of the future perfect after *si*, when the principle clause is in the future (*si dixerint...intelligent*), therefore in the Latin tradition.

---

[29] In the codex Bob. of the gospels, the perfect is often used in certain cases where the Vulgate has the present: e.g. *beati qui persecutione(m) passi sunt*, Mat. 5, 10 (οἱ δεδιωγμένοι). Moreover, perfects with the meaning of a present are not rare in late Latinity: e.g. *credidi*, for *credo*, by analogy with *cognoui* (cf. Salonius, Vitae patrum p. 292). This *credidi* usually has an inchoative meaning: e.g. *credidisse contenti*, TERT. Bapt. 1, 'being content to believe'; *credidi* (ἐπίστευσα), Act. 4, 4, 'I became a believer, I believe'; *si haec, inquit, ita esse credidisti, surge*, RVF. Hist. 10, 3 (Momm. p. 962, 29; *credis*, Migne).

§234 **2.3.9** In Classical Latin, the potential of the past is expressed by the imperfect of the subjunctive: *uideres, crederes, etc*., one could see, believe, or one would have seen, believed. St. Augustine also uses this imperfect for expressing a potential of the present, not only with verbs like *possem* (rare in Classical Latin), but with others:

scire *cuperem*, Ep. 40, 9, 'I should like to know';

uenire *dubitarem*, Ep. 59, 2 (see syntax of conditionals).

Other comments about the use of tenses will be found in the syntax of subordinate clauses and in the syntax of the infinitive.

3 Use Of Moods

3.1 Indicative

§235 **3.1.1** The present and the future of the indicative sometimes have the meaning of a deliberative subjunctive (colloquial language):

tu es qui uenturus es? an alium *exspectamus*? VVLG. Mat. 11, 3, 'or must we wait for another?'

quid *faciemus* et nos? Luc. 3, 14.

§236 **3.1.2** The future can be replaced by the subjunctive in maxims:

in procinctu semper *erit*, qui barbaros prohibere contendit, CASS. Var. 2, 5;

and the imperative in the commandments:

non occi*des*, VVLG. Ex. 20, 13; et passim.

These uses are not strangers to Classical Latin, and we have drawn attention to them in the use of the future [§228].

§237 **3.1.3** In the work of Tertullian principally, the future indicative can express certain shades of meaning normally translated by the subjunctive:

ostendemus, Apol. 10, 'one will show, one would show';

erit, Prax. 27 et passim, 'will be or would be';

haec *erunt* exempla, Iei. 16 (ταῦτ' ἂν εἴη παραδείγματα);

medici *considerabunt*, An. 14, 'the physicians will see, that the physicians discuss the question, it is the business of the physicians';

cf. uiderint, in the use of the subjunctive [§243],

si habens imperatorem alterum *appelles*, nonne maxime et inexorabilem offensam *contrahes*? Apol. 54, you would not commit...?'

(for the confusion of the future and the subjunctive present, see §235 and §244);

cf. quantis eum adflixerit poenis, humanus sermo non poterit explicare, VICT.-VIT. 3, 27.

§§238 **3.1.4** The imperative is replaced in certain manuscripts with the indicative:

dicis (= dic), ITAL. Mat. 18, 17 (cod. Palat.);
offers (= offer), Mat. 5, 24 (cod. Amiat.); Luc. 5, 14 (cod. Cant.);etc.
credis (= crede), HERM. Past. 6, 1 (cod. Vatic.).

§239 **3.1.5** One will see later the use of the moods in subordinate clauses; but, by way of an example, one can notice here alternations of subjunctive and indicative in which the meeting of moods is subtle, for one must not be too quick to say that it is fortuitous:

creator...ubique laudatur, uel quod... *inchoauerit*...uel quod *adiuuet*, uel quod *impleat*...uel quod peccantem... iustissima damnatione pro meritis *ordinat*, AVG. Lib. arb. 3, 22, 65. (One can suppose that the writer expresses at first in the subjunctive the reasons that he has in his mind when he praises the Creator; then, by a kind of mental anacoluthon, he presents in the indicative another reason, namely the fact, vividly illuminated for him, of predestination (one praises God for such and such a reason...and even because he punishes).

Here are two independent clauses, coordinated, and yet in a different mood:

cur non breuiter *dixerit*: 'nos haeretico noncommunicamus,' sed *addidit* 'quantum in nobis...?', AVG. Bapt. 6, 22, 39.

Here again the underlying meaning can be explained: 'why would he not be able to say purely and simply, why not say...(possible eventuality in the past) but then he added...' the second verb expresses a fact. We have here an example of a quick and nervous style of controversy; to know how to play delicately with these two moods, the indicative and the subjunctive, is in the pure Latin tradition.

3.2 Subjunctive

§240 **3.2.1** The optative subjunctive is often used without *utinam*, which, moreover, is not contrary to classical usage:

cum sanctis pignoribus *fruaris* tranquillitate perpetua, imperator auguste, AMBR. Ep. 51, 17, 'with your noble children, enjoy, august emperor, a perpetual tranquillity';
quod felicibus *sanciatur* auspiciis, CASS. Var. 3, 12, 2.

It often appears in the prayers of the liturgy to express a request, a demand, or a supplication:

tua caritas *abundet* in nobis, SACRAM. LEON. p. 160, 18;

also, in competition with the imperative:

nobis indulgentiam *tribue*, ibid. p. 68, 7.

§241 **3.2.2** The optative is also expressed by *si* and the subjunctive; it is a Hellenism (with εἰ):

si cognouisses, VVLG. Luc. 19, 42, 'if only you knew'.

For *forsitan, fortasse* = ἄν, see the dictionary.

§242 **3.2.3** The subjunctive alone, without *siue*, can express contrary suppositions; it is an extension of the use of classical expressions such as *uelit* and *nolit*:

scierit, nescierit, AVG. C. Cresc. 2, 26, 32;
ascendas, descendas, C. litt. Petil. 2, 100, 230.

§243 **3.2.4** The subjunctive forms *uiderit* and *uiderint* are a formula of omission (used earlier by Cicero and Ovid, but absolutely):

quos (daemonas) *uiderit* cur censeat honorandos, AVG. Ciu. 8, 19, 'let him find out how it is necessary, according to him, to honor them (I leave it to him to straighten out this contradiction)';
uiderint qui per capillum odorantur, TERT. Apol. 42, 'it is a matter of those who perfume their hair';
uiderint quantum uobis ceteri gratulentur, CYPR. Ep. 54, 2.

§244 **3.2.5** Example of the present subjunctive, in place of the future:

cum autem uenerit quod perfectum *est*...integra atque expressa ueritate resplendeat, AMBR. Psal. 118, 3, 19 (cf. §233).

In other cases, it is a matter of confusion of conjugation (§63).

7 Subordinate Object Clauses

1 The Personal Construction

§245 This construction [AG 582] which, in Classical Latin, is limited to the verbs *dico, trado, fero,* and analogous verbs, as well as to *iubeor, uetor,* and *uideor*, is extended to a larger number of verbs:

animalia quae Iudaeis *prohibita sunt manducare*, AVG. Serm. 149, 3, '...whose flesh has been forbidden to the Jews';
praecipimur rationem *reddere*, VICT.-VIT. 2, 56 (and often with this verb);
neque...negare arbitrandi sumus, HIER. Pelag. 1, 1, 'one ought not believe that we deny';
si quis...*inuentus fuerit non habere* uestem nuptialem, In Mat. 3, 22, 11;
ut *ostendatur* nec populus *esse* sine culpa, In Ier.2, 5, 30;
cum mendax *esse clarueris*, LVCIF. Athan. 2, c. 920, 'as your lies became patent';
quae *uiuere negari* non possunt, MAMERT. (Eng. p. 43, 2);
cf. with *sustineor*, CYPR. Ep. 30, 8; *scior*, ARN. 1, 34; etc.;

§§even with an accusative in the infinitive clause:

uidebar mihi ueluti iuniorem esse factum, HERM. Past. 9, 11.

2 Infinitive Clauses

§246 **2.1** The use of the infinitive clause with verbs making an assertion or expressing an opinion continues in the period of Late Latin; but in the Christian writers, it loses ground to the construction with *quod, quia,* or *quoniam*, as we shall see later.

§247 **2.2** On the other hand, the infinitive clause is found:

2.2.1 with verbs expressing desire and will, more often than in Classical Latin, which constructs them ordinarily with *ut* and the subjunctive:

opto omnes in ecclesia *regredi*, CYPR. Ep. 69, 16;
qui *claudos* praecipiebat *incedere*, ARN. 1, 63;
ceteros abire praecepit, HIER. Vit. Hilar. 22 (and often with this verb);
petiit *sese deponi*, VICT.-VIT. 3, 28.

§§In these constructions, the use of the gerundive constitutes a pleonasm, which occurs rather frequently in a not-so-refined time:

abbatem suo *decreuimus priuandum* officio, GREG.-M.Ep. 5, 4, c.725.

2.2.2 with verbs expressing fear:

metuebant *eos seduci*, AVG. Ep. 149, 24.

See in Chapter 10 the use of the infinitive alone with verbs expressing fear, will, and hope.

With these last constructions, the writer is content sometimes with the present infinitive in place of the future:

sperans *liberari*, BARNAB. Ep. 1, 3;
aestimantes *ossa inueniri*, EVGIPP. Vit. Seu. 44, 6.

§§248 **2.3** Infinitive clause with impersonal verbs or expressions:

nisi omnino *clareat*...nostra potius *esse certamina*, CASS. Var. 3, 2;
factum est episcopum ordinari, VICT.-VIT. 1, 24.

§249 **2.4** *Facio*, followed by the infinitive clause, can have the meaning of *iubeo*:

fecit oppidum claudi, ARN. 5, 7;
quem a diuersis indicibus *fecimus...perquiri*, CASS. Var. 5, 34;

or that of *facere ut*:

ecce Pater *fecit Filium nasci* de uirgine, AVG. Serm. 52, 9;
barbaros cum barbaris *fecit decernere*, AMBR. Ep. 24, 8.

§§250 **2.5** *Scilicet*, followed by the infinitive clause, in TERT. Marc. 4, 34, means 'apparently' ('it goes without saying that', in Plautus, Terence, and Lucretius).

3 Object Clauses with *Ut, Quominus,* and *Ne*

§251 **3.1** It is found, contrary to Classical usage, with verbs making an assertion or expressing an opinion:

censere ut, CYPR. Sent. 74;
credere ut, TERT. Marc. 3, 18; HIER. Ep. 106, 1;
audire ut, FILASTR. 132, 3;
spero ut, ALCIM. p. 86, 31;
asserere ut, CASS. Var. 2, 9; etc.

§§252 **3.2** These examples of *ut* before an infinitive clause never belong to carefully-composed language:

debemus fidem nostram *exprimere ut* haereticos...*debere eos baptizari*, CYPR. Sent. episc. 4 (these texts are not by Cyprian);
adnuntiantes uobis ut ab his uanis *conuerti* ad Deum uiuum, ITAL. Act. 13, 16 (cod. Laud.)(εὐαγγελιζόμενοι ὑμᾶς ... ἐπι στρέφειν);
euenit ut...hoc *dici*, HIER. Tr. psal. p. 170, 19 (familiar treatises);
persuadebat *ei...ut...communia esse* omnibus fidelibus reputare, THEOD.-MOPS. In ep. ad Phil. 17;
cf. monitione docemur *ne* cum delinquentibus... *uesci*, PS.-CYPR. Aleat. 5 (variant *ne quidem uesci*).

This use of the indicative is also a vulgarism:

fiebat ut omnis...ibat, ITAL. Ex. 33, 7 (ap. LVCIF.).

§253 **3.3** *Vt* with *iubeo* is rare in Classical Latin:

CYPR. Ep. 16, 4; 69, 13; VVLG. Gen. 42, 25; etc.

§254 **3.4** One finds likewise with this conjunction verbs like *promittere* and *iurare* (infinitive clause in Classical Latin):

quod *promisisset* Dominus...*ut* traderet, VVLG. Ios. 9, 24; CASS. Var. 8, 5;
iurauit patribus *ut* daret, Ex. 13, 5; iurare ut non, Deut. 4, 21; iurare ne, Gen. 21, 23.

§255 **3.5** As well as numerous impersonal expressions which would be accompanied by the simple infinitive in Classical Latin:

facilius est ut, AVG. Ciu. 21, 9 (earlier in Pliny the Younger);
difficile est ut, CAES. AREL. Serm. (Morin p. 219, 13);
tantum est ut, CASS. Var. 1, 31, 'it is enough that';

or which would be constructed with *quod*:

additur ut, CAES.-AREL. p. 563, 13, 'one adds that...'

§256 **3.6** *Vt* is found even in a negative clause:

ut nihil, HILAR. Psal. 13, 1 (cf. supra: *iurare ut non*);
caue ut non delinquas, COMM. Instr. 2, 5, 7.

For the construction of each verb, you must consult the dictionary.

§257 **3.7** The subjunctive is found alone with the expression *opus est*:

refrenes opus est, AVG. Ep. 12; Serm. 38, 25 (earlier in Pliny the Younger);

with *sinere*:

sinite illos *refrigerent*, PASS. PERP. 13.[30]

§258 **3.8** *Vt*, in place of *quominus*, with verbs expressing hindrance:

ut de ecclesia ueniant retardari, CYPR. Ep. 73, 24.

On the other hand, in this writer negative *deesse* is constructed with *quominus* or *quod*:

nec spiritu, *nec* actu...*defui quominus* fratribus nostris consulerem, Ep. 20, 1;

deesse non potest *quod* peccetur, Op. et el. 18, 'one cannot refrain from sinning'.

§259 **3.9** *Quominus*, in place of *ne* with verbs meaning 'fear'[31]:

quid in me tirone *timeat quominus* uelit sermonem conferre non satis intelligo, AVG. Ep. 36, 6, 'I do not really understand why, in an argument, he does not dare pit himself against a novice such as me' (see later *timere quod*; and in the dictionary under the word *quominus*, which will be found constructed with all kinds of verbs).

§260 **3.10** With *absit* 'far be it from us that, we do not accept that', one finds more often *ut* and the subjunctive:

TERT. Apol. 37; AVG. Serm. 214, 4; etc.;

but sometimes the subjunctive without *ut*:

CYPR. Ep. 33, 1:

or even the infinitive:

Ep. 30, 2.

4 The Object Clauses with *Quod*,[32] *Quia, Quoniam, etc.*

One of the remarkable characteristics of Christian Latin is, in accordance with the imitation of the the Greek ὅτι or ὡς, the use of *quod, quia, quoniam,* and even *qualiter, quatenus, quomodo,* with the indicative or the subjunctive, in place of the infinitive clause, with verbs making an assertion, expressing an opinion or feeling, etc. Our writers use the infinitive clause with the same verbs without a difference in meaning.

---

[30] Notice also in the Vulgate this absence of subordination:

factum est autem in diebus illis, exiit edictum, Luc. 2, 1 (ἐγένετο δὲ...ἐξῆλθεν δόγμα);
factum est autem...et ipse stabat, Luc. 5, 1.

[31] *dubitare ne*, CASS. Var. 8, 3, means 'fear that'.

[32] *Quod* is even found before an infinitive clause, e.g. *congaudere quod nos...pacem fecissee*, ap. CYPR. Ep. 53; VICT.-VIT. 3, 14; MAMERT. St. an. 1, 25; HIER. Tr. (Morin. Anec. III, 2, p. 406, 8); cf. *intellegendum quia... hoc dici*, Tr. in Is. p. 98, 7. It is a matter of an anacoluthon belonging to colloquial langauge.

A clause with *quod* coordinated to an infinitive clause, e.g. *accepimus eum esse consultum et quod responderit...*, AVG. Bapt. 3, 3, 4.

§261 **4.1** With *quod*:

4.1.1 in the indicative:

dixisti...quod in te *uiuimus*, AVG. Conf. 7, 9;
credimus quod illi...non potuerunt, Bapt. 1, 4, 6;
dico enim uobis quod multi prophetae *uoluerunt* uidere quae..., VVLG. Luc. 10, 24;
scimus quod de terra Deus *plasmauit* hominem, HIER. C. Iaon. 21; cf. In Is. 17, 60, 15;
Dominum praedicasse quod in fine mundi...*refrigescet* caritas..., Ep. 52, 4.

4.1.2 in the subjunctive:

4.1.2.1 scio quod...*operuerit*, Ep. 130, 2:
4.1.2.2 unde scire poterat Cain quod fratris eius munera suscepisset Deus, Qu. Hebr. Gen. p. 8, 16;
4.1.2.3 praedicasse continuo quod Iesus *esset* Filius Dei, In Gal. 1, 1, 17;
4.1.2.4 nuntiat Saluatori quod mater sua et fratres *stent* foris, In Mat. 2, 12, 4; Ep. 108, 18; VVLG. Gen. 22, 20;
4.1.2.5 ... de paganis diximus...quod persecutionem ab imperatoribus *patiantur*, AVG. Bapt. 1, 10, 16;
4.1.2.6 non puto quod...*debeamus*, SALV. Gub. 1, 2, 6;
4.1.2.7 puto quod...*cognoscas*, Gub. 1, 9, 40, 'I think that you ought to learn...';
4.1.2.8 declamas quod...nullam poenam *senserit*, MAMERT. St. an. p. 31, 21 ('according to you');
4.1.2.9 considerantes ac scientes quod (and subjunctive), CYPR. Hab. uirg. 2.

In most of these examples, the use of the subjunctive justifies itself, either because it expresses a subjective shade of meaning (3, 7, 8), or because the principle verb is in the negative or interrogative form (2, 6). It is natural that *praedicare*, in the sense of 'proclaim', may be followed by the subjunctive, but by the indicative when it is equivalent to *praedicere* (as in the last example of 1). On the other hand, in examples 1, 4, 5, and 9, it is more difficult to account for this mood, which has a tendency to encroach on the indicative in clauses of this kind; one will easily give an account of them by consulting the editions provided with an index. Just as the Classical writers say *gaudeo quod ualeas*, in competition with *gaudeo quod uales*, without thinking formally of a subjective shade of meaning, so we say in French *je ne crois pas qu'il soit venu*, as well as, *je ne crois pas qu'il est venu*, without formally intending to express a stronger doubt; likewise, in Late Latin, the subjunctive with *quod* became a use that was somewhat mechanical.

Sometimes *quod* is omitted:

denuntiantes eis, si manserint, capientur, EVGIPP. Vit. Seu. p. 42, 7 (cf. some analogous parataxes, footnote 30).

Other examples of the construction with *quod*, with verbs meaning 'permit':

polliceri quod (and subjunctive), CYPR. Ep. 73, 22;

with *non dubito*:

CAES.-AREL. Serm. (Morin, p. 66, 28): VVLG. Tob. 7, 13; etc.;

with a verb of feeling:

confido quod (and subjunctive), CASS. Var. 8, 11;

with a verb meaning 'fear':

timere quod (and subjunctive), HIER. Ez. 7 (at the end);

with an impersonal expression:

satis est quod omnia et facta a Deo constat et..., TERT. Herm. 33, 'it is enough for us to say that...'

plus est quod (and indicative), An. 19, 'there is, besides, the fact that...';

melius est quod (and indicative), CASS. Var. 11, praef.

§262 **4.2** With *quia*, which is more often followed by the indicative:

an *ignoratis quia* in morte ipsius baptizati sumus? VVLG. Rom. 6, 3:

audierat de te *quia* doceas, ACT. 21, 21;

non est dubium quia diligit, AVG. Serm. 15, 1;

uides...quia non potes, SALV. Gub. 2, 5;

scriptum est de ecclesia *quia* erit et uidetur quia est, CAES.-AREL. Serm. p. 596, 28;

dictum est a Deo *quia aspiciat* iugiter omnem terram, SALV. Gub. 3, 4;

cf. credo quia, TERT. An. 57; apparet quia, Adu. Marc. 4, 10.

§263 **4.3** With *quoniam*, most often followed by the indicative:

ignoras quoniam benignitas Dei ad paenitentiam te adducit? .VVLG. Rom. 2, 4;

in Actis apostolorum *inuenimus quoniam...*, TERT. Bapt. 10;

scire quoniam, CYPR. Eccl. un. 17;

ignorare quoniam, HIER. Ep. 147, 1.

§264 **4.4** Notice that these conjunctions in the Vulgate, just as ὅτι in Greek, can introduce direct discourse, thus being equivalent to the French colon [or the English comma]:

iurauit illi quia *dabo*, Marc. 6, 23;

confessus est quia *non sum* Christus, Io. 1, 20;

cf. coepit docere eos quoniam oportet (= oporteret), Marc. 8, 31 (ἤρξατο διδάσκειν ... ὅτι δεῖ; in Greek, one can have the same tense as in direct discourse);

§§and in the literature of translation:

praesignificabant...prophetae *quoniam uidebitur* Christus, IREN. 4, 20, 5;

cf. repromissionem *acceperat quia* in semine tuo *benedicentur*, HIER. Tr. I in psal. p. 9, 9.

§265 **4.5** The following conjunctions are used more frequently:

4.5.1 *qualiter*:

dixit...*qualiter* populus...uoluisset, VVLG. Iudith, 6, 12, 'he told how..., he said that';

scitis...*qualiter* uobiscum per omne tempus fuerim, Act. 20, 18.

§266 **4.5.2** *quomodo*, always with the indicative (C.-AVR.):

intelligitis quomodo in parabolis posita sunt multa, BARNAB. Ep. 17;

uiderunt oculi tui *quomodo* (ὡς; VVLG. quod) tradidit te Dominus, ITAL. 1 Reg. 24, 11, ap. LVCIF. Athan. 1, 14;

recordamini quomodo distracta sunt, OPTAT. 3, 10;

cf. dicam uobis quemadmodum..., VIT. PATR. 3, 212 (= 5, 12, 9 quia: δεικνύω ὑμῖν ὅτι).

In these examples it is not a matter of indirect questions.

§§267 **4.5.3** *quatenus* 'that', followed by the subjunctive: HADR. I Ep. 5, 3, c. 1211. As in the case of *quod*, we find this conjunction in adverbial clauses of purpose, cause, and result; it is particularly common in Medieval Latin.

§§268 **4.5.4** *plus est si*, followed by the indicative: TERT. Pud. 9, 'it is still taking one more step if...';

sufficit si, Adu. Marc. 2, 26, 'it is enough that'.

§§269 **4.5.5** Notice the biblical expressions with *iurare si*, with a negative meaning:

iuraui in ira mea, si introibunt, VVLG. Ps. 94, 11, 'I indeed swore that they would not enter';

iurare nisi, with an affirmative meaning;

iurauit per semitipsum dicens: nisi benedicens benedicam te et multiplicans multiplicabo te, Hebr. 6, 13 and 14 (Gen. 22, 16), 'he swore...that he would bless...'.

5 Indirect Questions

§270 **5.1** In Late Latin, the indicative mood often replaces the subjunctive in clauses of this kind; this usage, moreover, was not unknown in Old Latin:

quomodo infructuosi *uidemur*... non scio, TERT. Apol. 42, 'I do not see why one regards us as useless';
si scire uultis quid *facitis*, AVG. Serm. 196, 4;
intellige quid *loquitur*, HIER. Pelag. 3, 8;
nesciens quod de illo *decreuerat* Deus, VICT.-VIT. 1, 31;
considerandum est quid aetate eminenti iam dignum *est*, PS. CYPR. De duod. abus. 2, 'that must be understood which is suitable to an already advanced age';
putas ubi mittendus *est*, qui inuasit alienam (rem), CAES.-AREL. Serm. p. 595, 16, 'imagine, where will he be sent who...?'

Notice this alternation of mood:

scis *quis sum* ego? et ille dixit: Deus te scit *quis sis*, VIT. PATR. 5, 15, 66 (there is, no doubt, more vividness in the first clause in the indicative).

§271 **5.2** During the Empire, *an* introduced a simple indirect question after verbs other than *nescio* and *dubito*, for example, *spectare* and *quaerere*; later this usage was developed even more:

examinare an, CYPR. Mort. 16;
cum cognoscitur *an mereatur*, TERT. Apol. 1, 'when one knows if (this thing) is worth it'.

This adverb can also replace *utrum*:

ut probetur *an* uerum dicit, *an* mentitur, AVG. C. Fel. 1, 55;
nec interest talibus *an sumere* cibum, *an sustinere* ieiunium, CASS. Var. 11, 10, 1 (for this use of the infinitive, see 5 below).

§272 **5.3** In classical poetry, the indirect question introduced by the adverb *si* occurs only after verbs like *mirari*; in our time period, one finds it after other verbs, notably *uidere*:

uidete si est dolor sicut dolor meus, VVLG. Ier. lam. 1, 12;
uideamus si non resistunt, AMBR. Ep. 40, 9;
uideamus si haeretici describuntur in psalmo illo, AVG. Bapt. 6, 31, 60;
si quid passi estis *nescio*, C. litt. Petil. 2, 8, 20 (but in this writer, *si* and the subjunctive with the classical meaning of 'if, in the case where');
qui episcopus ordinandus est, antea *examinetur si* natura sit prudens, CONC. CARTH. IV, cap. 1 (Ma. 3, c. 949);
perpendite, patres conscripti, *si* hanc subolem inremuneratam relinquere debuimus, CASS. Var. 2, 16;

and in a double indirect question:

si...an (non), LVCIF. Non parc. 19;
si...siue non (εἰ...ἢ οὔ), ITAL. Deut. 8, 2 (Roensch, p. 404).

Examples of a triple question:

utrumne...an...seu, CASSIAN. Coll. 1, 20, 2;

utrum...ue...seu, Inst. 8, 6.

§272b **5.4** The interrogative adverb *ne* can be non-enclitic in a direct or indirect question:

ne tu maior sis? ITAL. Io. 4, 12, ap. TERT. Marc. 4, 35 (μή);
(with the indicative) AVG. Ciu. 1, 28; AMBR. Psal. 37, 26;
audire ne, ARN. 1, 10, and AVG. Ep. 193, 4, 10, 'to learn if by chance';
nescio ne, TERT. Nat. 1, 10.
uidere ne, Carn. Chr. 23, 'to see if' (in Classical Latin, *uidere ne* means 'to see to it that...not', (*ne* being the conjunction);
recogitare ne, Apol. 2;
cogitauit ne posset, VICT.-VIT. 3, 50, 'tried if she could not';

even with the meaning of *nonne*:

uideamus ne hic honor ad totam respiciat trinitatem, FAVST.-R. Spir. Sc. 1, 7, p. 112, 22;
cf. TERT. Apol. 26.

§273 **5.5** One finds even the infinitive in an indirect question:

istos nescire quid *loqui*, AVG. Ep. 157, 4, 27;
nescire quod *dicere*, C. litt. Petil. 2, 51, 118;
non inueni aliud qua *transire*, ap. EVGIPP. Exc. p.381, 8;
non habebamus ubi *requiescere*, HIER. Tr. I in psal. p. 61, 1;
nescit quo *flectere* puppem, CORIP. Ioh. 1, 273;
quidnam *deliberare* ambigebant, IORD. Get. 25, 131.

8 Subordinate Adverbial Clauses

Preliminary remarks

§274 In studying the use of moods (section on the indicative, at the end [§239]) and subordinate object clauses with *quod* [§261]), we observed that the underlying meanings separating the subjunctive and the indicative continued to be felt in Late Latin, except that in certain situations the subjunctive arose without any apparent reason. The same thing happens in the syntax of adverbial clauses, where one even sees the subjunctive come into competition with the indicative in the same sentence, in two coordinated or juxtaposed clauses.

cum subuenerit nemo et plena *sunt* omnia..., ARN. 1, 49;

cum Esau primatus suos... *perdidit* nec recipere potuerit, CYPR. Ep. 73, 25;

quod a Deo *recessistis* et pro illo uos idola *delectarunt* et *fornicatae sitis*, HIER. Ier. 1, 3, 12;

quando peccant...et recesserint, ibid. 2, 9, 10;

quid erit suauius quam...protulisse iudicium, ubi tot patriciorum corda *prouocantur* ad gratiam, *ubi* bonum factum *celebretur* ore sapientium? CASS. Var. 3, 11.

Furthermore, in certain cases, the indicative takes the place of the subjunctive, contrary to classical usage, for example, with *cum* causal; in other cases, it is the subjunctive which occurs, for example, in concessive clauses introduced by *quanquam*; one will find the details of this in the paragraphs which follow.

1 Causal Clauses

§275 **1.1** Classical Latin uses the subjunctive after *quod*, more rarely after *quia*, when the cause is presented, not as a fact, but as the thought or the speech of the subject of the main clause. There is an analogous distinction with verbs of feeling.

By analogy with these last distinctions, St. Jerome uses the subjunctive with *flere*:

fleuit et Dominus super ciuitatem Ierusalem, quia non egisset paenitentiam, Ep. 122, 1. It is a question of a fact (Jerusalem had not done penance), but presented as the thought of the Master.

The following sentence is another example of this tendency to introduce everywhere the subjunctive with a verb of feeling:

in hoc habui *consolationem* quod *fuerit*..., In Ier. 3, 15, 17.

In the following example the subjective shade of meaning is less apparent:

Pythagorae igitur, *quia* nihil ipse *scriptitauerit*, a posteris quaerenda sententia est, MAMERT. St. an. 2, 3, 'since Pythagoras did not write anything, one must search for his thought in the disciples whom he has left (this is not only a fact that Claudianus Mamertus records, it is also what researchers themselves say);

ipse autem Iesus non credebat semetipsum eis, *eo quod*[33] *nosset* omnes, VVLG. Io. 2, 24; the subjunctive here expresses the underlying meaning of indirect discourse: I am acquainted with them, he was thinking. (As the gospel of St. John appears among the texts of the New Testament which are reshaped by Jerome and not merely retouched, one must see in it an intended meaning by the Latin translator; moreover, there is not an optative in the Greek text διὰ τὸ αὐτὸν γινώσκειν).

§276 **1.2** In Classical Latin, the construction *non quod...sed quod* is constructed with the subjunctive in the first clause and the indicative in the second; this distinction is not always observed in our writers:

non enim...ista accidunt quod dii uestri a nobis non colantur, *sed quod* a vobis non *colatur* Deus, CYPR. Ad Demetr. 5;

non quod ipse esset Pater et Filius, *sed quod* tam similes *sint*..., AVG. Tr. eu. Io. 70, 2; HIER. Ier. 3, 14, 2.

Inversely, *non quia* occurs followed by the indicative:

non...quia in martyribus *reperitur* (uirginitas), *sed quia* ipsa martyras *faciat*, AMBR. Virg. 1, 3, 10; cf. LVCIF. Athan. 2, c. 889 A.

§§277 **1.3** Example of *quoniam* before an independent clause, with the meaning 'because':

quoniam quis audiuit? VVLG. Ps. 58, 8; Ps. 8, 2.

§278 **1.4** *Cum* causal occurs with the indicative in place of the subjunctive:

[33] There is also *pro eo quod*, followed by the infinitive (Classical Latin *propterea quod*): VVLG. Ps. 108, 15; *ipsum quod* (with the indicative), TERT. Prax. 9, 'for the same reason that'.

cum propriis filiis Saturnus non *perpercit*, TERT. Apol. 9, 'Saturn not having spared his own children';
cum eum argumenta *deficiunt*,...in luxurias epularum...invehitur, AVG. Ep. 36, 2, 3, 'short of arguments, he was angry at the sumptuousness of the banquet' (it is not a question of a habitual action).
quem tibi terribilis concussit corde pauorem uisus, *cum* laeti sermonis gratia *placat*? IVVC. 1, 15 (*cum* 'when' moves easily from the temporal meaning to the causal);
cum dierum noctiumque uices *variant*, MAMERT. St. an. 2, 12;
cf. CASS. Var. 2, 28.

§279 **1.5** Already in Sallust, Livy, and others, *quando* followed by the subjunctive has taken on a causal meaning 'since, from the moment that'. It became very frequent in the Christian writers:

quando aliud baptisma praeter unum esse non *possit*, CYPR. Eccl. un. 11;
cf. TERT. Prax. 29; Apol. 1; Nat. 1, 16; AMBR. Luc. 5, 5; AVG. Ep. ad cath. 3, 6; FAVST Trin. praef.; etc.

§280 **1.6** To express cause, our writers use some conjunctions that do not have this meaning in Classical Latin:

1.6.1 *Quare* 'since':

ferte praesidium ut expugnemus Gabaon, *quare transfugerit* ad Iosue, VVLG. Ios. 10, 4;

Quare 'because':

tumeant contra me mariti *quare dixerim*, HIER. Ep. 48, 15;
arguatur euangelista mendacii, *quare addiderit*, Ep. 57, 7.

In these different situations, Classical Latin would use *quod* and the subjunctive.

1.6.2 *Quomodo* 'since':

TERT. Prax. 15.

1.6.3 *Vt* 'considering that':

ut meminisset nostrum se esse doctorem, AVG. Tr. eu. Io. 104, 2 (Classical Latin *ut qui eminisset*, or else *ut meminerat*);
pro eo ut 'for the reason that': VVLG. Ps. 108, 16.

1.6.4 *Quatenus*: 'since, from the moment that', followed by the subjunctive (earlier in HOR., PLIN.-I. TAC.): TERT. Prax. 17; Herm. 32; SVLP.-SEV. Dial. 1, 12, 5; MINVC. 5, 6.

§281 **1.6.5** *Dum* 'from the moment that, since', followed by the indicative:

dum non redditur (baptismus), amitti non potuisse iudicatur, AVG. Bapt. 1, 1, 2;

magno et mirabili aequitatis iure certatum est, *dum* omnipotens Deus...in nostra *congreditur* humilitate, LEO-M. Serm. 21, 1, '...since the omnipotent Lord fought (as He was fighting) after having assumed our own frail nature'.

medendi peritus inuitum frequentur saluat aegrotum, *dum* uoluntas recta in grauibus passionibus *non est*, CASS. Var. 1, 5, '...because (rather than 'when') in serious illnesses the will is no longer normal';

cf. TERT. Apol. 29; Adu. Marc. 4, 8.

It seems that writers may have departed from the classical meaning of the explanatory *dum*, which can be translated in English by 'while' and the present participle [in French by *en* and the present participle]. Certain sentences show an intermediate meaning:

Iudaei nonne inde perierunt, *dum* Christo *malunt* inuidere quam credere? CYPR. Zel. 5, '...while preferring, while they preferred, because they preferred'.

In other cases, *dum* expresses more the manner or the means:

nos reparat, *dum* quod cecidit in Adam primo *erigitur* in secundo, LEO-M. Serm. 12, 1, 'he redeems us, while rising in the second Adam...';

dum humanam conditionem sideribus *importauit*, PS.-AVG. Serm. 176, 1, 'while transporting humanity to the heavens';

non quia peccat homo *dum moritur*, AVG. ap. EVIGIPP. Exc. p. 279, 8, not that death be a sin for man (see the temporal clauses, 3, §311).

Less often, this *dum* causal is followed by the subjunctive unless the underlying meaning expressed is different:

dum eos detestaretur, AVG. Vnic bapt. 13, 22, 'because he detested them';

nec tardari...uolumus...*dum uelimus* omnia inter nos esse decisa, CASS. Var. 1, 23, 2, 'it is not to wish to drag things on at length that we desire' (see, in the temporal clauses, *dum* in place of *cum*).

§282 **1.6.6** *Siquidem* or *si quidem* 'since, considering that', followed most often by the subjunctive, in place of the classical indicative:

LACT. Inst. 4, 14, 17; HIER. C. Lucif. 20; SVLP.-SEV. Chron. 2, 3, 6; Dial 2, 6, 6.

1.7 *Quo* 'because', with the indicative:

hoc ipso operari amplius debes, *quo* multorum pignerum pater *es*, CYPR. Op. et el. 18, 'good works are all the more a duty for you because you are the father of many children' (Classical Latin *eo magis quod*, when the second clause does not contain any comparatives; the grammars also classify these constructions in the comparatives).

1.8 *Cur.* The classical poets offer some examples of *irasci cur.* In the Christian writers, it became a conjunction which is used with verbs expressing accusation or protestation:

detrahere alicui cur, HIER. Ep. 27, 1, 'to reproach someone for';
argui cur, PS.-AMBR. Serm. 58, 'to be accused of';
de hoc queruntur cur ita sit positum, FILASTR. 130;
frendes cur fuisset admissus, SVLP.-SEV. Dial. 2, 5, 8.

One finds it even followed by the indicative:

dolore cor nostrum repletum est *quur* bonitas uestra nos audire *renuit*, STEPH. II p. 492; BON. II c. 37 B.

2 Final Clauses [Purpose Clauses]

§283 **2.1** In negative clauses, *ut non* very often replaces *ne*:

sed fugerunt *ut non uiderent* te uidentem se, AVG. Conf. 5, 2, '...in order not to see that you see them';
ut non cadam, VVLG. Eccli. 22, 33; Ps. 9, 42; CAES.-AREL. Serm. p. 76, 4; etc.;
cf. cur pergis ad eremum...? *ut* te *non* audiam,...*ne* me capiat oculus meretricis, HIER. C. Vigil. 16;

likewise one finds:

ut nullus in place of *ne quisquam*: CASS. Var. 2, 8;
ne...et non in place of *ne...neue*, ibid. 7, 15.

§284 **2.2** *Quo* is used sometimes in place of *ut* even when the clause does not contain a comparative, which is rare in Classical Latin:

rogabam te...*quo sanares* dolorem meum, AVG. Conf. 2, 12; 6, 13; 8, 13; TERT. Apol. 27; 47.

§285 **2.3** Certain conjunctions express purpose in a way contrary to Classical usage:

2.3.1 *Quatenus* 'so that up to that time, in order that':

quatenus ueniente Domino mereantur audire, PS.-CYPR. Duod. abus. 10; RVF. Orig. princ. 4, 1, 19; INNOC. Ep. 3, 1; AVG. Catech 14, 21; CASS. Compl. in Rom. 35; PS.-AMBR. Serm. 1, 38; GREG.-M. Past. 3, 29.

2.3.2 *Quemadmodum* 'so that, in order that': CASS. Var. 7, 2; 12, 3.

3 Consecutive Clauses

§286 **3.1** *Ne* can replace *ut...non*: TERT. Carn. Chr. 3; SALV. Eccl. 3, 64; MAMERT. p. 33, 19;

ideo ne, TERT. Apol. 47.

§287 **3.2** *In tantum ut* 'to such a point that' appears earlier in Seneca:
in tantum nihil possunt cultoribus suis ut..., HIER. Gal. 2, 4, 8, 'they are so far from being able to do something for their worshippers that...'.

But this expression is found later, meaning 'so that':
CAES.-AREL. Serm. p. 502, 1; p. 547, 13.

§§288 **3.3** *Vt* 'to the point of' is found followed by an infinitive clause:

ITAL. 2 Cor. 2, 1, ap. TERT. Pud. 13; Act. 15, 39 (cod. Cant.) (= ὥστε and the infinitive).

§§289 **3.4** *Ita...quo* 'in such a manner that' with the subjunctive:
EVGIPP. Vit. Seu. p. 56, 19.

§§290 **3.5** *Quatenus*:
sed uide ut tantum doctrinae deferas quatenus probabiliter minia perquisitus exponas, CASS. Var. 6, 5, 'enough knowledge to be able to explain to him...';
et sic...quemadmodum 'so that' with the subjunctive: Var. 7, 2.

§291 **3.6** What is more remarkable is to find consecutive clauses in the indicative:
ita ut nihil efficiebat fame et siti, LVCIAN. ap. CYPR. Ep. 22, 2;
ecclesia...ualde pulchra...ut uere digna est domus Dei, PEREG. 19, 3;
especially with conjunctions other than *ut*:
quo hic iturus est *quia* non inueniemus eum? VVLG. Io. 7, 35, 'where will he go so that we should no longer be able to find him' (ὅτι ἡμεῖς οὐχ εὑρήσομεν);
sic...quod: SID. Ep. 3, 3; SALV. Gub. 7, 22, 96; MAMERT. St. an. 2, 9;
ita...quod: SALV. Gub. 1, 3, 15; 7, 21, 89; SID. Ep. 3, 13;
tantum...quod: SALV. Gub. 7, 23, 107.

§292 **3.7** Of course *quod* consecutive can also be followed by the subjunctive:
in populos quoque praefati imperatores similiter saeuientes *quod* eis nec donandi nec testandi (facultas)...penitus *subiaceret*, VICT.-VIT. 3,9, 'the said emperors so cruel toward their people that the latter no longer had any power to make a donation or a will'.

§293 **3.8** In place of *dignus qui*, one encounters *dignus ut* (earlier in LIV. and QUINT.):
non sum dignus ut soluam, VVLG. Io. 1, 27; AMBR. Ep. 10, 8.

But this adjective is constructed most often with the infinitive as in classical poetry or Seneca:

quae legi digna sunt, HIER. Ep. 74, 6;
dignos Deum nosse, TERT. Apol. 18;
dignus audire, CYPR. Ep. 21, 1.

4 Concessive Clauses

§294 **4.1** *Cum* concessive is found followed by the indicative in place of the subjunctive:

cum in forma Dei aequalis *est*, tamen per formam serui..., AVG. Ep. 140, 28, 68;
cur non uultis uera esse...cum...centum episcopi iudicauerunt, C. Cresc. 4, 7, 9.

§295 **4.2** *Quanquam* is constructed sometimes with the subjunctive in Vergil, Livy, and Tacitus; it became current usage in Late Latin:

quanquam ego *habeam* confidentiam, VVLG. Philipp. 3, 4; MINVC. 14, 3; TERT. Val. 39; CYPR., Ep. 12, 2; 30, 5; HIER. Ep. 14, 5; 22, 8; Vit. Hil. 1; SVLP.-SEV. Chron. 1, 2, 1; AVG. Ciu. 17, 5; etc.

This conjunction can be found before a noun, forming a kind of ellipsis (in Cicero only before a participle or a gerundive):

quanquam debellator Iudaeorum, TERT. Apol. 5, 'although the destroyer of the Jews that he was'.

§296 **4.3** *Etsi* constructed with the indicative and indicating opposition is more rare than *quanquam* in Classical Latin. It is found in our writers.

etsi a Numa Pompilio *concepta est* curiositas superstitiosa,...tamen..., TERT. Apol. 25, 'if it is true that it is Numa who created the superstitious fervor';
etsi homines ipsos minus *nouimus*, AVG. Parm. 2, 2, 4.

The subjunctive (earlier in Justin) is also used without the underlying meaning being noticeably different:

etsi idem *sentiant*, MAMERT. St. an. 1, 1;
etsi a corruptis et adulteris *habeatur*, AVG. Bapt. 4, 2, 2.

A similar lack of difference with *etiamsi*:

etiamsi mali fuerunt, Parm. 1, 4, 6;
etiamsi ostendant, ibid. 1, 11, 18.

By analogy with *quod si*:

quod etsi...sequimini, PETIL. ap. AVG. C. litt. Petil. 2, 56, 127.

§297 **4.4** *Licet* is constructed with the subjunctive in Classical Latin; Christian writers use either mood:

licet noster homo *corrumpatur*, VVLG. 2 Cor. 4, 16; Gal. 1, 8;
licet legimus, AMBR. Ep. 60, 9; CYPR. Ep. 8, 2; FAVST. Trin. 2, 13;
licet nostra iussa...in nullo uiolanda *sunt*, CASS. Var. 1, 25;

but the last writer prefers the subjunctive.

This conjunction is used in an elliptical way, before an adjective or an adverb in Ovid and Seneca. In Christian writers it is found before a participle:

reluctanti *licet*, CYPR. Laps. 25, 'in spite of her resistance';

before a noun:

licet hostem, AVG. Parm. 1, 11, 1, 'although the enemy';
licet haereticum, C. Cresc. 3, 50, 55;

before an ablative absolute:

licet meritis nequaquam suffragantibus, P.-AQVIL. Ep. p. 513; PASS. FRVCTVOSI 4.

§298 **4.5** *Quamuis* is used sometimes in Classical Latin with the meaning of 'although' with the indicative, and more rarely with the subjunctive; this usage becomes more frequent:

quamuis tria milia ascenderant, AMBR. Ep. 19, 21;

with the subjunctive:

FILASTR. 127, 2; LEO-M. Serm. 19, 1.

Before an adjective *quamuis* means 'however'; in Christian writers it is found before a participle or an ablative absolute:

et ipsa, *quamuis creata*, sapientia, AVG. Conf. 12, 15, 'although created as she is';
quamuis absentibus nobis, Conf. 9, 3, 'in spite of our absence'.

§299 **4.6** Other conjunctions express opposition:

4.6.1 *Qvando* 'when' with a meaning intermediate between the underlying causal meaning and the concessive:

nec iugum necessitatis imponit, *quando maneat* uoluntatis arbitrium liberum, CYPR. Hab. uirg. 23;

more rarely with the indicative:

uel ex uobis discant, quando docere debuerant, Ep. 15, 2, 'when they would have been obliged to teach him';
cf. *quando* 'since however, although': TERT. Prax. 11.

4.6.2 *Quamlibet*, in place of *quamuis*:

quamlibet sis multo comitatu stipatus, MINVC. 37, 9, 'whatever be the number of your retinue'.

§300 **4.6.3** *Dum* 'when however':

eam (ecclesiam) se habere, *dum non haberet*, putabat, AVG. Bapt. 5, 20, 28;
dum...interim 'although yet, when':
TERT. Apol. 42; AVG. Peccat. merit. 1, 33, 62;

dum...tum: 'although...nevertheless':
dum cuncta negotia sollicitudine *indigeant, tum* (haec) sunt distinctius trutinanda, GREG.-M. Ep. 3, 8, 'although all the matters claim our attention, these ought to be examined more particularly';
dum 'whereas, if':
nihil refert integram abire corporis nauem, an dissipatam, *dum* animae nauigatio *euertatur*, TERT. An. 52, 'no matter if the ship of the body departs, intact or broken up, if, unhappily, it is the soul that is shipwrecked'.
with the indicative:
dum debueratis, GREG.-M. Ep. 7, 39, 'when you should have had'.

§§301 **4.6.4** *Donec* 'provided that':
EVGIPP. Vit. Seu. 3, 4.
4.6.5 *Tantum...Non* 'provided that...not' followed by the subjunctive:
AVG. Catech. 11, 16.
4.6.6 *Pro eo ut* 'in place of' followed by the subjunctive:
VVLG. Ps. 108, 3.

§302 **4.7** The indefinite relatives are followed by the subjunctive, contrary to Classical usage, which demanded the indicative (a usage parallel to that of *quanquam*):
ubicumque sit paradisus, AVG. Ep. 187, 3, 7. See the dictionary under the words *qualiscumque, quisquis, quicumque.*

5 Conditional Clauses

§303 **5.1** The subjunctive is used in place of the indicative to express a habitual action in the past:
non enim *discerem*, nisi *cogerer*, AVG. Conf. 1, 12, 'I would learn only if constrained and forced'.
The following example calls to mind the temporal causal clauses in *cum* used to express a habitual action (in the time of Livy):
si suos...culpabiles *repperisset*, oculos eis *iubebat* erui, GREG.-T. Hist. 4, 46.

§304 **5.2** One finds often enough the indicative in the main clause [the apodosis] and the potential mood or unreal [i.e. contrary-to-fact; see GL 597 and AG 514] in the subordinate clause [the protasis or if-clause]:
5.2.1 Future indicative [in the main clause]:
si...sapienter...*intelligamus*...*inueniemus*, LEO-M. Serm. 12, 1, 'supposing we can understand...we will see';
quae enim *dabitur* discordantibus pax, *si* nec legitimis *adquiescant*? CASS. Var. 1, 5.

Although Classical Latin uses the future in this situation in the conditional clause [the protasis or if-clause], it also provides examples of the potential subjunctive (*si fractus illabatur orbis, impauidum ferient ruinae*, HOR. Od. 3, 3, 7). This usage is not illogical; moreover, it ought to be compared with what we have said about the use of the moods, i.e. about the relationship which exists in Latin between the present subjunctive and the future indicative. But the following uses are more daring.

§305 **5.2.2** Present indicative [in the main clause]:

non tamen regnum caeleste *consequitur,...nisi recte*...gradiatur, CYPR. Eccl. un. 15, 'he does not necessarily reach the kingdom of heaven...unless he walks on the right path';

si quaeras, subiciunt;...si reposcas, adiciunt, MAMERT. St. an. 1. 1, '...if you pose a new question, they still say...';

si robora primis scintillis *adhibeas*, igniculum *opprimis*, CASS. Var. 1, 40, 'let us suppose that one starts with the first sparks, [then] he has only a small fire to overcome'.

§306 **5.2.3** Imperfect indicative [in the main clause]:

nam concupiscentiam *nesciebam, nisi* lex *diceret*: non concupisces, Rom. 7, 7, 'I would not know concupiscence if the law did not say...'.

In a sentence of this sort, the indicative in Classical Latin would mean that the eventuality was on the point of being realized; it is almost the case here, because the Greek text does not have ἄν (οὐχ ἔγων). On the other hand, in the following example the imperfect indicative corresponds closely to a Greek imperfect with ἄν (οὐκ ἔγων) expressing the unreal [i.e. contrary-to-fact; see GL 597 and AG 514]:

si esset nunc iudex, peccatores non *erigebantur*, HIER. Tr. (Morin, Anec. III, 2, p. 44), 'would not rise, would not be able to rise' (Vulgar Latin, see below the example of Gregory of Tours).

As in Classical Latin, the indicative is used with verbs or constructions expressing possibility, fitness, and obligation, and in this way the two moods still alternate:

bonum erat ei, *si* natus non *fuisset*, VVLG. Mat. 26, 24, 'it would have been better for him..'.;

dimitti *poterat* homo hic, *si* non[34] *appellasset* Caesarem, Act. 26, 32, 'he would have been able to be released..'.;

and even with other verbs in a Latin style that is not so refined:

si domus mea digna esset, praestare non *abnuebam*, GREG.-T. Hist. 1, 31, 'I did not refuse, I would not have been able to refuse'.

---

[34] *Si non* is found in some contexts where Classical Latin used *nisi*: CAES.-AREL. Serm. p. 612, 18 and even two negations: *nisi non cessauerit*, ibid. p. 179, 13.

5.2.4 Perfect indicative [in the main clause]:

arcem..., *nisi* obsisterem, *proposuistis* obruere, ENNOD. Opusc. 2, 99, 'if I did not oppose it...';

si ullus *esset* consulendi modus...digne *meruimus*, AVG. Ep. 90.

§307 **5.2.5** Pluperfect indicative [in the main clause]:

euaserat Cecilius pondus uerecundiae, *si...genuissent*, CASS. Var. 8, 12, 'he would have avoided the disgrace, if the preceding centuries had produced...';

nihil *fecerat, nisi* curam faciendi *habuisset*, antequam faceret, SALV. Gub. 4, 42;

tantum uirum persona non *grauauerat, nisi* causa *multasset*, ibid. 2, 15.

In Classical Latin, the pluperfect would express the underlying meaning of action almost accomplished in the past (*perierat, nisi*...); but here they correspond simply to an aorist with ἄν expressing the unreal of the past.

§308 **5.3** In the subordinate clause [the if-clause], one finds sometimes:

5.3.1 the imperfect subjunctive, when the meaning is potential and when it is a matter of a possible eventuality (for the same use in the main clause, see use of tenses, 9):

si domum nostram quisquam diues... *intraret*, omni festinatione domus nostra mundaretur, GREG.-M. Hom. eu. 30, 2;

5.3.2 the imperfect indicative (a Hellenism) when it is a matter of the unreal [i.e. contrary-to-fact; see GL 597 and AG 514]:

et utique, *si* id (idolum) *colebatur*, TERT. Apol. 16 (now the Jews do not do it) (for the same use in the main clause, see above, 2.3).

5.4 *Nisi quia*,[35] *nisi quod*, (εἰ μὴ ὅτι) 'was only the fact' are used with the indicative (PL.): *nisi quia Dominus adiuuit me*, VVLG. Ps. 93, 17;

nisi quod lex tua meditatio mea est, tunc forte periissem, Ps. 118, 92; Gen. 3, 11.

6 Temporal Clauses

§309 **6.1** In Classical Latin, if one speaks of a past event, the subjunctive is used with *antequam* or *priusquam* when it is a matter of expressing intention or expectation on the part of the subject of the main clause. In our time period, the subjunctive tends to be used almost exclusively whereas in the classical period the subjunctive with a purely temporal meaning is rare.

[35] Lucifer (Lucifer Calaritanus), Bishop of Cagliari, uses the subjunctive in this construction: *neque...Danihel leones et tres pueri uincerent ignes, nisi quia credentes fuissent*, Athan. 1, 41.

priusquam de animae substantia *decernat*,... disputat, MAMERT St. an. 2, 3, 'before having dealt with the essence of the soul, he discusses...'.

The subjunctive here is not absolutely contrary to the classical usage, if one wishes to make it understood that the interlocutor has taken care beforehand 'to deal with the essence of the soul'; but in the following examples it is a matter of pure occurrence of time:

antequam idola *essent*,...*idolatria* transigebatur, TERT. Idol. 11;
antequam Christus *ueniret* in carnem, FILASTR. 107, 3;
ab aeterno ordinata sum et ex antiquis, *antequam* terra *fieret*, VVLG. Prou. 8, 23;
priusquam montes *fierent*,...tu es, Deus, Ps. 89, 2;
ubi Dominus auditus est, *antequam pateretur*, ITIN. BVRD. p. 22, 23, 'before his passion';
ecce *prius* culpas ignoscimus, *quam* deuotiones aliquas *sentiamus*, CASS. Var. 10, 13.

§310 **6.2** An important point to note is the retreat of *cum*, in favor of other conjunctions, especially *dum*.

One encounters the latter conjunction with the imperfect subjunctive, with the meaning of *cum*.

6.2.1 Either to express an event which happened at the same time as another, at a particular moment:

dum rogaretur, EVGIPP. Vit Seu. p. 5, 7, 'as one questioned him' or 'while one questioned him';
dum illi *turbarentur*, effugit, VVLG. Iud. 3, 26, 'during their confusion', or, 'taking advantage of their confusion';
dum irent emere, uenit sponsus, Mat. 25, 10;
dum irem Damascum..., uidi, Act. 26, 12;
euangelica lectio... *dum legeretur*, audiuimus, CEAS.-AREL. Serm. p. 562, 2.

In several of these examples, it is certainly less a matter of a temporal causal clause than of a clause expressing simply simultaneity; but, in any case, if Classical Latin gave up using *cum* and the subjunctive in this case, it would be *dum* and the indicative which it would choose.

6.2.2 Or to express an event which was recurring or lasting:

inueterauerunt ossa, *dum clamarem* tota die, VVLG. Ps. 31, 3;
dum essem adulescens, HIER. Ep. 52, 1;
dum morarer in Syria, Vit. Mal. 2.

§311 **6.3** *Dum* is also used with the meaning of *cum* 'when':

6.3.1 either with the subjunctive (in indirect discourse):

Achior dixit...ut, *dum uicerit* filios Israel (Holoferenes), tunc et ipsum Achior...iubeat interire, VVLG. Iudith 6, 13, 'told...how (Holofernes), when he should have conquered (Classical Latin *cum vicisset*) the sons of Israel, would put [Achior] himself to death'.

6.3.2 or with the indicative:

quis est qui non euangelium recognoscat, *dum cantatur* ille psalmus, AVG. Ep. ad cath. 8, 21, 'when it is sung, each time that it is sung' (rather than 'while it is sung');

ut, dum sibi...fratres uicissim *succedunt*, sciat, BEN. Reg. 32, 'so that he might know each time that the brothers have to make use of it in turn'.

In these examples, it is a matter of a habitual action.

In the following, *dum* expresses also an underlying meaning of manner or of means;

noli me uerberare sermonibus, *dum dicis*, EVGIPP. Ep. p. 2, 18, 'while speaking';

sicut imperasti, *dum* discipulorum fidem *roborasti*, PASS. XII AFR. p. 140, 'when you strengthened, while strengthening';

quos incognitos cogitur accusare, *dum* separationem suam *conatur* defendere, AVG. Parm. 3, 4, 20, 'when he tries, while trying to defend';

dum se uidit (diabolus) ceteris potiorem, inflatus est ad exercendam dominationem, PS.-AVG. Qu. test. 98, 1, 'while seeing himself (Classical Latin *cum se uidisset*) (compare this example with *dum* causal).

It is also used with the meaning of *cum* and the imperfect subjunctive:

ubi ait Dominus 'ignem ueni mittere in terram', *cum* de Spiritu Sancto *diceret*, MAMERT. St. an. 1, 14, 'while speaking, when he spoke about the Holy Spirit' (Classical Latin *cum dicebat*).

§312 **6.4** With *donec*[36] also the classical distinction between the subjunctive and the indicative tends to disappear, the first being used most, even with the meaning 'until':

inueterascensira fit odium...*donec* totum aces*cat* atque corrum*pat*, AVG. Ep. 38, 2;

non tamen segregabantur ab illis qui aliter celebrabant, *donec* Romanae ecclesiae Victor episcopus excommunicationem...*misisset*, CASS. Hist. 9, 38, 'until the time when he had sent, as long as he had not sent'.

Donec means also 'while waiting for the moment when':

hoc ergo donec fiat, da nobis ueniam, AVG. Ep. 91, 2.

---

[36] For *donique* and *denique*, see the dictionary.

§313 **6.5** In accordance with the extension of the use of the subjunctive in temporal clauses, *postquam* is found followed by this mood, even after a previous indicative:

postquam uenerabiles episcopos *remisimus* nec petitionibus uestris... noster animus *obuiasset*, CASS. Var. 10, 13.

§314 **6.6** *Quamdiu* in Classical Latin means 'as long as, during all the time that' and it is followed by the indicative; in our time period, it means 'until,' and it is most often followed by the subjunctive:

non cogitare nec scire...noctem tamdiu esse *quamdiu inlucescat* dies, CYPR. Ep. 59, 11; CASSIAN. Coll. 14, 13; VICT.-VIT. 1, 10.

It means also 'as many times as' with the indicative:

quamdiu fecistis uni ex his fratribus meis minimis, VVLG. Mat. 25,40.

§315 **6.7** Various conjunctions or conjunctive expressions express the time, contrary to classical usage:

§§ *Quomodo* 'when':
ITAL. 2 Reg. 8, 29, ap. LVCIF. Athan. 1, 34.

§§ *Quoniam* 'when':
TERT. Virg. uel. 3.

§§ *Quotiens* (= *cum* expressing a habitual action):
BEN. Reg. 3; CASS. Var. 1, 15.

Diu est ut 'it is a long time ago that' with the indicative:
AVG. Spir. et litt. 13, 21, or *diu est quod* (PL.); CASS. Var. 9, 18.

Mox ut 'as soon as':
VVLG. Ps. 36, 20; AVG. Conf. 9, 4.

Quo usque 'until':
AVG. C. part. Don. 8, 11;

or as a single word:

Quousque ad nos redeas,
GREG.-M. Ep. 8, 6; AVG. Conf. 11, 2; Symb. 4, 1; CASSIAN. Inst. 10, 7, 1; Coll. 23, 12, 6;

more rarely with the indicative 'up to the moment when':
AVG. Conf. 2, 4.

This conjunction still means 'as long as':
A.-VICT.; M.-EMP.

Quod appears also in temporal clauses in place of *cum* or *ex quo* 'when, since':

tempus est quod nobis praestet auxilium, HIER. Ez. hom. 11, c. 805 A;
plures anni sunt quod, Ep. 77, 1;
biduum hodie est quod, Vit. Hil. 29;
triginta annos habeo quod non deprecor, VIT. PATR. 5, 4, 39.

7 Comparative Clauses

§316 **7.1** Tertullian uses *quod* in a comparative clause with the meaning 'such as, as' (= *ut*); the verb is understood or expressed:

manante impetu, *quod angues...*, quod uermes, An. 10, 'by gliding, as snakes, worms (which snakes do)';

ludos...Libero deuotos, *quod sunt* Dionysia penes Graecos, Spect. 10;

before a participle (= *tanquam*):

cum alicuius defuncti recordaris, misellum eum uocas, non utique *quod* de bono uitae *ereptum*, sed ut poenae et iudicio iam adscriptum, An. 4, '...not certainly as torn away from the joy of living, but as already under the blows of punishment and of judgement' (one can also in this example see especially an underlying causal meaning).

See later, in the relative clauses, *quod* explanatory; and in the dictionary the adverbs *quantum, quam, qua,* and *tanquam.*

§§317 **7.2** Notice *ante...quam*, with the meaning of *potius quam*:

GREG.-M. Ep. 1, 16 a.

Cicero sometimes uses *priusquam* with this meaning.

8 Relative Clauses

§318 Here also one sees the ancient distinctions between the indicative and the subjunctive little by little disappear. The latter mood was used in Classical Latin when the relative expressed an adverbial meaning; in the following example the two relative clauses are in a different mood for no apparent reason:

pater...summa fuit morum nobilitate conspicuus, quem nec feruentia bella *respuerunt* et tranquilla otia *praedicarent*, CASS. Var. 8, 17, '...in the fire of war, he did not fall in contempt and the tranquillity of peace saw him famous'.

§319 **8.1** The indicative can be used with *sunt qui* (earlier in Classical Latin, when *sunt qui* was equivalent to *quidam*):

sunt qui pauperibus paulum *tribuunt*, HIER. Ep. 52, 9; CYPR. Eccl. un. 10; AMBR. Ep. 64, 90.

See in the consecutive clauses the construction of *dignus.*

§320 **8.2** Examples of relative clauses in the indicative, although expressing an underlying causal meaning:

sciebant et Iudaei uenturum esse Christum, *scilicet quibus* prophetae *loquebantur*, TERT. Apol. 21, 'because the prophets were speaking about it to them';

beata...quae *credidisti*, VVLG. Luc. 1, 45;

with *utpote qui*:

VICT.-VIT. 2, 49.

With *quippe qui*, St. Jerome always uses the indicative, some examples of which one finds earlier in Sallust. An underlying conditional meaning:

iam nec reuelator ipse erit, qui absconditor non *fuit*, TERT. Marc. 4, 25, '...if he were not first hidden'.

§321 **8.3** On the other hand, the subjunctive is found where Classical Latin would not have any reason for using it: thus *constat*, in a relative clause, is always in the subjunctive in Cyprian:

quomodo possunt duo aut tres in nomine Christi colligi, *quos constet* a Christo et ab eius euangelio separari, CYPR. Eccl. un. 12, 'when it is established that they are separated'.

One can understand there an underlying causal meaning; but not in this sentence:

quod utique ei dicitur quem constet cecidisse, Ep. 55, 22.

cf. steti in sententia mea illa qua caderem, ENNOD. Op. 5 (Hart. p. 399, 23).

§§322 **8.4** Some relative clauses are found in the infinitive, to express an underlying consecutive meaning (popular construction);

ut habeat quem semper uisitare, AVG. Serm. (Morin, p. 416, 10).

§323 **8.5** The relative *quod* is used in an elliptical manner with the meaning 'that is to say, such as':

pontifex scilicet maximus, *quod episcopus* episcoporum, TERT. Pud. 1;

in diuersitate sublimitatis eminentiae, *quod leonis*, uituli, hominis et aquilae, FILASTR. 132, 2.

For *de cuius* and *in quo*, see the dictionary.

9 Sequence of Tenses

§324 **1.** Certain departures from the rule of sequence of tenses can be explained in accordance with the Classical tradition:

ipse te instituitut *sapias*, AVG. Serm. 344, 7;
scripsisti ut tibi...recit*etur*, C. Cresc. 2, 27, 33;
consider*aui* omnes epistulas tuas, ut uiderem quarum responsionum debitor *sim*, Ep. 11, 1.

Instituit, scripsisti, and *consideraui* are perfects expressing action accomplished, result achieved at the present time; moreover, the present *sim* naturally means that he, at the present time, owes these responses.

In the following sentence:

qui nascitur ut ostend*eret*, GREG.-M. Hom. eu. 8, 1,

nascitur can be considered as a historic present (see, also, the following paragraph).

§325 **2.** The imperfect subjunctive seems to express a future eventuality, which is unknown in Classical Latin (Classical Latin uses an imperfect subjunctive after a main verb in the present only when the meaning demands it, either to express the unreal [i.e. contrary-to-fact; see GL 597 and AG 514] or to call up a situation that was continuing in the past:

haec *scribo* ut agnosceres, HIER. Ep. 22, 3;
daemones postul*ant* ut mitterentur, Tr. in psal. p. 54, 17;
opti*net* ut... *deferretur*, SVLP.-SEV. Chron. 2, 49, 3;
eius dextera *eligitur* ad sacrificium ut *moreretur*, AVG. Serm. 2, 1;
credentes quod nihil *eueniret* aduersi, EVGIPP. Vit. p. 27, 13;
timeo ne *diceremus*, SALV. Gub. 4, 30;
id ipsum persequitur nullam faciens mentionem, ne quisque *sentiret*, MAMERT. St. An. 1, 12, 'would not happen to notice':
me ad te petis ut *scriberem*, AVG. Ep. 20, 3.

Evidently also when the main verb is in the past tense:

cum utique et ipse dixerit Deus quod cum ipso *esset* ('he would be with him') ut fuit cum Moyse et eum similiter *illuminaret* ('he would enlighten him'), AMBR. Psal. 17, 27.

Magis inquirentibus *ubi* Christus *nasceretur*...respondebant, AVG. Serm. 201, 2.

In this example:

dedit folles uiginti ut *factus esset* presbyter, AVG. C. Cresc. 3, 29, 33, it is still a matter of the future (*factus esset* = *fieret*); at this time, it is possible that *factus esset* might seem less a pluperfect than *factus fuisset*.

§326 **3.** In certain cases, the absence of proper sequence cannot be explained:

haec idcirco replica*uimus*...ut stud*eamus*, HIER. Ep. 100, 8;
quid mansuetius *sit* quam ut...*multaretur*, AVG. C. litt. Petil. 2, 83, 184;
mirari *possim* quod hoc non omnes *facerent*, SALV. Gub. 5, 38;
in sua domo *maluit* sepeliri...ut...alienam se a filio nunquam esse *confidat*, VICT.-VIT. 3, 24.

With regard to the confusion of the imperfect subjunctive and the pluperfect subjunctive, see the use of tenses.

10 Infinitive

By an evolution already begun in the poets of the classical period, one finds this mood commonly used in place of a gerund, of a gerundive of a *supine*, of a clause with *ut*, of a relative clause (after *dignus*), etc.

§327 **1.** Modifier of a noun [*complément du nom*] in place of a gerund in *-di*:

occasio non *habere*, TERT. Cast. 10, 'the occasion of not having';
potestatem infirmos *curare*, HIER. Mat. 1, 10, 7;
consuetudinem *corrigere*, AVG. Bapt. 2, 7, 12, 'the habit of correcting'.

§328 **2.** In place of *ad* followed by the gerund in *-dum*:

(animalia) nihil *nata* sunt *prospicere* nisi pabulum, MINVC. 17, 2 (cf. HOR. Ep. 1, 2, 27).

§329 **3.** In place of a gerundive:

mandasti mandata *custodire* nimis, VVLG. Ps. 118, 4.

§330 **4.** Frequently in place of a supine[37] dependent on a verb of movement:

erumpunt *dicere*, TERT. Marc. 1, 17, 'they burst out saying';
abiit *quaerere*, BEN. Reg. 27;
sanare uenit aegrotum, AVG. Tr. eu. Io. 12, 12;
exiit in montem *orare*, VVLG. Luc. 6, 12;
non uenti iustos *uocare*, sed peccatores, HIER. Ep. 11;
et satiatus accessit de aqua *ludere*, PASS. PERP. 8, 'to play with water'.

---

[37] The supine is rare in the works of Christian writers: e.g. the supine in *-um* expressing purpose: *potum dare*, VVLG., Mat. 10, 42; the supine in *-um* after an adjective: *necessarius cognitum*, MAMAERT. p. 24, 6; the supine in *-u* after a phrase (rare in Classical Latin): *fas est dictu*, HIER. Vit. Pauli 3; PRVD. Apoth. 822.

§331 **5.** Infinitive of purpose, even after other verbs (a Hellenism):

exsurget regere gentes, VVLG. Rom. 15, 12 (ἀνιστάμενος ἄρχειν);
dare ad manducare, ITAL. Io. 6, 52 (cod. Verc.);
sedit manducare, VVLG. Ex. 32, 6;
nobis *tribuens* uitam habere cum Christo, HIER. Ephes. 1, 2, 1;
Deus qui sine concubitu apes *fetare creauit*, PS.-AVG. Hypomn. 4, 7, 13;
dicere quaerebaris, CASS. Var. 8, 12, 3, 'you were asked to say'.

§332 **6.** The infinitive in place of *ut* with the subjunctive is used more often than previously with verbs expressing effort or will:

impetrauit implere, TERT. Iei. 7;

with *monere*:

Pud. 20;

with *niti*:

CYPR. Laps. 22; with *hortari*: Ep. 8, 2;

with *suadere*,

HIER. Ep. 100, 8;

with *monere*,

C. Ioan. 39 (earlier in Cicero, occasionally);

with *persuadere*:

CASS. Var. 5, 14;
custodire laboremus, CAES.-AREl. Serm. p. 126, 20.

See the dictionary for each verb.

This infinitive is found normally with verbs of will which previously expressed opinion:

Adam et Eua... pudenda *tegere senserunt*, TERT. An. 38, 'felt the need of hiding':
credidit *sociare*, VICT.-VIT. 1, 30.

§333 **7.** In place of *ne* and the subjunctive with verbs meaning 'fear':

metuo, HIER. Ep. 14, 10 (earlier in PL., HOR.):
timeo 'to hesitate to': noli *timere accipere* Mariam coniugem, VVLG. Mat. 1, 20.

§334 **8.** With *ualeo* and *praeualeo*, with the meaning of *possum*:

requiem *inuenire non ualeat*, HIER. Is. 7, 23, 13.

§335 **9.** In place of *ut* consecutive:

o insensati Galatae, quis uos fascinauit *non oboedire* ueritati, VVLG. Gal. 3, 1.

§336 **10.** The infinitive modifying an adjective is frequent in the poets and writers of the Empire, likewise in our writers:

potens *formare*, AVG. Conf. 9, 6, 'capable of forming';
dignus *soluere*, VVLG. Luc. 3, 16;
stultus *damnare*, HIER. Tr. p. 422, 11, 'crazy to the point of condemning'.

§§337 **11.** Infinitive, in place of the imperative (a Hellenism):
gentes autem super misericordia *honorare* Deum, VVLG. Rom. 15, 9, 'as for the Gentiles, they have to praise God for his pity';
orationi *insistere*, uigilantes in ea cum gratiarum actione, THEÓD.-MOPS. Col. 4, 2.
12. Infinitive in an indirect question (see §273).

§338 **13.** The perfect infinitive, in place of the present,[38] occurs in classical poetry after verbs of feeling and in prose after verbs like *possum, uolo, decet*, and *oportet*. Later this use is further developed, and the perfect infinitive has only the force of the Greek aorist infinitive.
possum antitheses *retudisse*, TERT. Marc. 1, 19, 'I can refute (I can have finished refuting)';
sanguinem...*fudisse* parati sumus, CYPR. Ep. 31, 5, 'we are ready to shed all our blood';
ausi sunt *superbisse*, Ep. 3, 1;
after *lucuit*:
AMBR. Tob. 5, 22;
potuit *dixisse*, AVG. C. litt. Petil. 2, 102, 235;
adhaesisse *iurasti*, VICT.-VIT. 1, 11;
nequaquam metuunt ueritatis *fecisse* iacturam, MAMERT. St. an. 1, 1
praeconiorum ergo professio est collegium *desiderasse* summorum, CASS. Var. 4, 25, 'it is honorable to want to be a member of the great ones';
after *uideri* (which forms, moreover, a pleonasm, see §222 and §223):
ne... utilitati publicae uoluptas priuata *obstitisse* uideatur, CASS. Var. 5, 17.

§339 **14.** The present infinitive is used, in place of the future, after verbs meaning 'promise, predict', or 'hope for':
praedictum est..., adpropinquante Antichristo, bona quaeque *deficere*, mala uero et aduersa *proficere*, CYPR. Ep. 67, 7;
TERT. Marc. 3, 18; LACT. Ep. 65, 5; COMM. Instr. 1, 28, 2;
nisi promittis mihi *dare*, VVLG. Tob. 7, 10;
certus neminem *refutare* doctorum, MAMERT p. 122, 1;

[38] The opposite is more rare: e.g. the present in place of the past, *martyria quam plurima esse probantur*, VICT.-VIT. 1, 30.

et ea die speratur *reuerti* ad monasterium, BEN. Reg. 51;
si promiserit se omnia *custodire*, ibid. 58.

§340 **15.** The infinitive as noun is very common; it is an extension of the classical use of the infinitive as subject, predicate, or object:

Christum uidere *gaudere* est, CYPR. Mort. 5, 'it is a joy to...';
ipsum *uelle* substantia est, MAMERT St. an. p. 86, 12;
sic sum ipsum *esse*, sic sum cum ipso *esse*, AVG. Serm. 7, 7, '...I am with being itself';
quid impossibile ei qui dedit *posse* infirmis, AMBR. Hex. 2, 3, 11;
quae, dum sunt, habent *posse*; et dum possunt, habent *esse*, TERT. Praescr. 2, 'as long as they exist (the heresies), they have the power (of causing faith to die); and as long as they have this power, they have existence';
ad suum *uelle* festinat, CASS. Var. 6, 15, 4.

One finds it even preceded by a preposition:

inter dici et esse, TERT. Nat. 1, 5 (μεταξὺ τοῦ λέγεσθαι καὶ τοῦ εἶναι);
ad manducare, ITAL. Io. 6, 52 (Verc.); ad offerre, Eccli. 45, 20 (Tolet.);
distantia inter facere et generare, FAVSTIN. Trin. 2, 14;
ut perueniatur *ad semper* uiuere, AVG. Disc. 1, 1;
nullum interest inter confirmare et facere, C. litt. Petil. 3, 53, 65;
cum ueneris *ad bibere*, Serm. 225, 4;
in moechando et idolothytum *edere*, IREN. 1, 27.

11 Gerund and Gerundive

1 The Gerund

§§341 **1.1** Without becoming current usage the gerund in *-do* occurs in place of the infinitive and seems to correspond to a Greek participle:

desiit loquendo, VVLG. 3 Esdr. 4, 41;
non desinis petendo, HERM. Past. 1, 1, 4;
cessare loquendo, ITAL. Iudith 5, 26 (cod. Corb.);
iterauit faciendo, PASS. ISAAC (M. 8, c. 771 B; 780 B).

§§342 **1.2** Moreover, any gerund can replace an infinitive subject or object:

qui *fruendum* Deo...unum atque summum bonum nostrum *esse* dicunt, AVG. Ep. 118, 3, 16, 'they say that the enjoyment of God is...';
secedendi...nulla ratio *sinebat* loci, VICT.-VIT. 2, 32, 'nothing in the layout of the area permitted one to withdraw oneself'.

§343 **1.3** In Classical Latin, the ablative of the gerund expresses the means or instrument; but from the beginning of the Empire, it expresses any circumstance [under which the action of the gerund occurs] and corresponds to a present participle:

orando ingemuerunt, VICT.-VIT. 2, 11;
nuncupauit dicendo, TERT. Pat. 11;
qui pertransiuit benefaciendo, VVLG. Act. 10, 38;
nec iam ingemescebam orando ut..., AVG. Conf. 6, 3;
philosophicam non intelligendo sententiam, MAMERT,p. 52, 21, 'not understanding, because you did not understand';
nunc age inhaerendo iustitiae, CASS. Var. 5, 3 (see the opposite usage in the chapter on the participle where a present participle is used in place of a gerund in *-do*).

§§In the Psalms, one even finds it with this meaning preceded by *in* (Classical Latin *in convertendis inimicis*, cf. 4):

in convertendo inimicum meum retrorsum, VVLG. Ps.9, 4;
in conveniendo populos in unum, Ps. 101, 22.

§344 **1.4** *Ad* and the accusative of the gerund followed by an object of the gerund [*complément d'objet*] is rare in Classical Latin, which normally replaces it with a gerund-and-gerundive construction [AG 503ff.] . On the other hand, it has become common among our writers, and this extension is perhaps due to Greek influence:

ad sanandum *eos*, VVLG. Luc. 5, 17 (εἰς τὸ ἰᾶσθαι αὐτούς);
ad declinandum *disciplinam*, TERT. Apol. 21, 'to deviate from the rule';
ad infuscandum *originem*, Res. 6;
scribere ad instituendum *alios*, AMBR. Ep. 64, 7;
ad persequendum *Hebraeos*, GREG.-T. Hist. 1, 10;
utendum seruitiis, VICT.-VIT. 3, 62.

§345 **1.5** The gerund preceded by *ad* can have a passive meaning, with an underlying implication of futurity or of destination:

sicut ouis *ad immolandum* ductus est, LACT. Inst. 1, 4, 'to be immolated';
et tradent eum gentibus *ad illundendum et flagellandum et crucifigendum*, VVLG. Mat. 20, 19;
scit apostolus nos derelinqui *ad tentandum*, HILAR. Psal. 118, 1, 15, 'abandoned to temptation'.

It has this meaning in the following example, where Classical Latin used the supine:

loca...grata *ad uidendum*, PEREG. 19, 5, 'agreeable to see (to be seen)'.

2 Gerundive

§346 **2.1** The gerundive in the neuter followed by an object [*complément d'objet*] occurs in Old Latin and postclassical Latin:

multa dicen*dum fuit*, TERT. Pall. 3;
Sardanapa*lum* tacen*dum* est, Pall. 4;
seniorem unum aut duos cum fratribus dimitten*dum*, BEN. Reg. 56.

§347 **2.2** The gerundive is often found constructed with an ablative of agent [*complément d'agent à l'ablatif*], in place of the dative:

et *a uobis* diuersitas (diuinitatis) *defendenda* est, TERT. Marc. 1, 16;
nihil...a iusto uiro faciendum est, LACT. Inst. 6, 12, 7; etc.

§348 **2.3** In Classical Latin, the gerund or the gerundive preceded by *ad* expresses purpose; this construction can be replaced in our time period either by *propter*:

propter molestias declinandas, AMBR. Ep. 17, 4;

or by *pro*:

pro iuuanda republica, CASS. Var. 1, 4, 11;

or by the dative:

latronibus uestigandis, TERT. Apol. 2, 'to search for the robbers':
nocentibus erogandis, Nat. 1, 10, 'to kill the criminals';
liberandis omnibus uenit, LEO.-M. Serm. 21, 1.

The dative can also express destination:

mappam, qua *tergendis manibus* utebatur, CASS. Var. 3, 51, 9.

§349 **2.4** The gerundive in Classical Latin expressed destination after certain verbs, such as *dare, curare, etc.* (*dare pueros educandos*). In Late Latin, it is used, as a predicate adjective or in apposition with the meaning of a future passive participle[39]:

Filius hominis *tradendus* est, VVLG. Mat. 17, 22, 'is to be handed over, will be handed over':

et forte *ducenda* (= quam ducturus es) amatur, ducta odio habebitur, AVG. Serm. 21, 1, 'and if that is found before the marriage, you love her; after, you will detest her;

quaeritur qui sit iste, qui *ducendus* sit in captiuitatem et ultra non *reuersurus*, HIER. Ier. 4, 22, 12; '...who will be led into captivity and will never return';

iuraui res illius a me esse *tollendas*, SALV. Gub. 5, 10;

retinemus sanctorum corpora angelicis *exaequanda* corporibus, MAMERT. p. 57, 15, 'will be assimilated into the bodies of angels' (and also: 'are destined to be angels');

confido enim quod per te *reddenda* sit (= fore ut reddatur) sanitati, SVLP.-SEV. Mart. 16, 4, 'I have confidence that through you she will be restored to health';

sacra *grauidanda* fetu, LEO.-M. Serm. 21, 1, 'this woman who had to carry...';

facienda erit discussio (= fiet), BEN. Reg. 2.

In several of these examples, the idea of destination is simultaneously present; in others, it is a matter of the simple future.

§350 **2.5** The gerundive can also express possibility (this occurs in Classical Latin only in negative sentences):

non magno molimine *refellendi* sunt, AVG. Peccat. merit. 1, 17, 22, 'one can refute them without great effort';

coniciendum est, Catech. 2, 3, 'one can infer, conclude'.

§§351 **2.6** It can even replace a present passive:

---

[39] St. Caesarius even uses the gerundive with the future, creating a kind of redundancy: *ubi mittendus erit*, Serm. p. 71, 21; *erimus offerendi*, p. 595, 16.

cum secanda est (= cum secatur), puncto caeditur, MAMERT. p. 90, 12 (compare the use of the future, in place of the present, by the same writer, §226).

12 Participle[40]

§352 **1.** The meaning of participles like *consistens, constitutus*, and *positus* was considerably weakened, and they mean only 'being, occurring':

fratribus in plebe *consistentibus*, CYPR. Ep. 17;
episcopis trans mare *constitutis*, Ep. 43, 3;
Paulo adhuc in carcere *posito*, Ep. 27, 1;
ego Tolosae *positus*, SVLP.-SEV. Ep. 3, 3;
in stadio *constituti*, AMBR. Hel. 22, 81, 'when we are at the stadium';
in rebus temporalibus *constituti*, FEL. II Ep. p. 13;
cf. TERT. Spect. 25; ARN. 5, 7; AVG. Peccat. merit. 2, 16, 24; etc.

§353 **2.** More often than in Classical Latin, the present participle is used with an adverbial force [*valeur circonstancielle*],

2.1 of time:

orantes autem, nolite multum loqui, VVLG. Mat. 6, 7, 'when you pray (προσευχόμενοι)'.

As in French, the present participle can have a passive meaning:

ueniens...uir uenerabilis declarauit, CASS. Var. 12, 26 (= *cum uenisset*, see below no. 4);

§354 **2.2** of manner or means:

delectabat eos *loquens*, AVG. Conf. 5, 6 (= *loquendo*);
signa multa *faciens* se Deum esse declarat, GREG.-T. (Bonnet, p. 650), 'by his many miracles...';

§§and in parallel with a gerund:

partiendo...et duodecim (psalmos) per unamquaque constituens noctem, BEN. Reg. 18;

§355 **2.3** of continuity:

---

[40] We have already pointed out the construction of the present participle with the verb *sum* (§225) and the absolute participle in the accusative (§76).

ibat proficiens, VVLG. Gen. 26, 13, 'he was going to grow rich' (cf. no. 3);

§356 **2.4** of cause:

peccaui *tradens* sanguinem iustum, Mat. 27, 4;

As in Greek ἅτε or ὡς, *ut* before a participle means 'as, in the thought of, being given that': TERT. Apol. 35; 41; 45 (before an adjective or a noun in Classical Latin);

§357 **2.5** of concession:

nullam causam mortis *inuenientes* in eum, petierunt a Pilato ut interficerent eum, VVLG. Act. 13, 28 (εὑρόντες);

§358 **2.6** of purpose:

sine uideamus an ueniat Helias *liberans* eum, Mat. 27, 49;
ite tollentes, Ex. 12, 21, 'go take':

§359 **2.7** of condition:

a quibus *custodientes* uos, bene agetis, Act. 15, 29;
nondum credentibus, CYPR. Dom. orat. 17 (var.), 'if they still do not believe'.

These are often Hellenisms.

§360 **3.** And as in Greek, the present participle is found in place of the infinitive after verbs expressing cessation or continuity:

cum *consummasset* Iesus *praecipiens*, VVLG. Mat. 11, 1 (ὅτε ἐτέλεσεν...διατάσσων);
si perseuerauerit *pulsans*, Luc. 11, 8;
cum desinerent *manducantes*, ACT. ARCHEL. 11, 4;
non prius destitit...orando et ieiunando *continuans*, SVLP.-SEV. Dial. 3, 13, 4.

Other examples of Hellenisms:

manifestus est labefactans fiduciam, TERT. Res. 31 (φανερός ἐστι σφάλλων);
praevenio admonens, Praescr. 9 (φθάνω ἀναμνήσας).

§361 **4.** Less attention is paid to the preciseness of tense, and the present participle[41] is used where one would expect a past tense:

---

[41] In certain instances, the present participle expresses a subsequent action: e.g. *conuocauit omnem populum illum dicens* (= *et dixit*), GREG.-T. Hist. 2, 40; cf. Juret, Filastr. 12; Goelzer, Avit. 294.

inuenientes pacatam prouiniciam,...depopulabantur, VICT.-VIT. 1, 3 (= cum inuenissent);
quod si tu *audiens* respondeas, BEN. Reg. prol;
benedicente abbate legantur aliae quatuor lectiones, Reg. 11, 'after the abbot's benediction...;
cum quadam die in proximo...uico *ueniens*...praecepisset, EVGIPP. Seu. 8;
Dauiticam *deserens* ciuitatem, uenerat..., SEDVL. Op. 4, 5.

§§362 **5.** On rare occasions, the future participle is found with a passive meaning:

uocati ad *recepturum* donum gratiae, PS.-AVG. Qu. test. 44, 2 (= ad recipiendum, ut reciperetur).

§363 **6.** The ablative absolute is sometimes used, even when the participle refers to the subject or to a word in the clause:

et *ascendente eo* in nauiculam, secuti sunt *eum*, VVLG. Mat. 8, 23;
me tecum *laborante*, non parum temporis *dedi*, AVG. Ord. 2, 3, 9;
statim *illis clamantibus includuntur*, VICT.-VIT. 2, 28;
dicatur hic uersus...ipso tamen incipiente, BEN. Reg. 38, 'Let this verse be recited,...the one which begins...'.

§§364 **7.** Some absolute participles are in the nominative and do not refer to the subject of the clause:

cognoscentes (nos) simulque legentes, contritum est extemplo cor nostrum, VICT.-VIT. 2, 40;
uexillo crucis *consignans* oculos eius, statim caecus uisum recepit, ibid. 2, 50, 'as soon as he (the thaumaturge) made the sign of the cross on his eyes, the blind man regained his sight;
talis est mos Dei cultoribus totum reseruare Deo, *scientes* esse magnum uindicari ab eo, LVCIF. Athan. 1, 14;
aestimet se homo de caelis a Deo semper respici...*demonstrans nobis hoc propheta*, BEN. Reg. 7 (cf. chap. 1, 1, 1).

§365 **8.** Certain ablative absolutes are formed from a past participle, such as *comperto* and *audito*, and a clause; this construction is found earlier in the historians Sallust, Livy, and Tacitus. In Christian writers, it is ordinarily used with a quod clause:

comperto quod homines essent sine litteris, VVLG. Act. 4, 13, 'having learned that...;
perlato sibi quod..., EVGIPP. Vit. Seu. 5.

§§366 **9.** In some very late writers, the noun or the pronoun which ought to be the subject of the absolute participle is its object [*complément*]; and the participle is then equivalent to a preposition governing the accusative:

completo matutinas, ANTON. Itin. 11;
foedus inito, IORD. Get. 21, 112;
quod comperto, ibid. 25, 132.

Appendix 1: Principal Spelling Variants*

To avoid overloading the dictionary with all of the variant forms, we give here a list of the principal spelling variants† that are found in the manuscripts, especially in the writers of the Merovingian period.

Vowels:

a for *e*:	*parantum (parentum)*
	consacrare (consecrare) (etymological reaction)
inversely:	*-erius (arius)*
a for *o:*	*datalicium (dotalicium)*
inversely:	*abbotissa (abbatissa)*
freq. *e* for *ae:*	*egritudo (aegritudo)*
	seculum, seclum (saeculum)
inversely:	*aeclesia (ecclesia)*
	praemo (premo)
	adfectuosae (adfectuose)
	in planitiae (planitie)
freq. *e* for *oe:*	*cenobium (coenobiam)*
freq. *e* for *i* (long or short):	
	sterelitas (sterilitas)
	iubeleus (iubileus)
	legare (ligare)
	certamine (certamini)
	-ebus (-ibus)
recomposition:	*assedente (assidente)*
	redemere (redimere)
inversely:	*diocisis (dioecesis)*
	ribus (rebus)
	iudix (iudex)

---

*[Appendix 1 is not included in Blaise's *Manuel du latin chrétien* but has been reprinted from the *Dictionnaire latin-français des auteurs chrétiens*, pp. 30-31].

† We do not mention here the variants that are found in the dictionaries, such as *adt-* for *att, adf-* for *aff-*, *tempt-* for *tent-*, *subp-* for *supp-*, etc.

prefixes *di-* and *de-* often confused:

-ia for *ea:*	*platia (platea)*
	dulciamina (dulceamina)
i for *e:*	*muneri (munere)*
	it (et)
	uellit (uellet)
	catechuminus (catechumenus)
i for *ii:*	*fili (filii)*
i for *y:*	*sinaxis (synaxis)*
	sticos (stychus)
inversely:	*cylicium (cilicium)*
	alymentum (alimentum)
i syncopated:	*aspicentes (aspicientes)*
	domne (domine)
i for *g:*	*aiebat (agebat)*
	iniens (ingens)
i for *oe:*	*obidientia (oboedientia)*
i added before an *s* followed by a consonant:	
	ispatium (spatium)
e added before an *s* followed by a consonant:	
	escrinium (scrinium)
ae, oe confused:	*praelium (proelium)*
	poenitentia (paenitentia)
oe for *e:*	*decoepistis (decepistis)*
o for *oe:*	*diocesis (dioecesis)*
o for *u:*	*puerolus (puerulus)*
	postolant (postulant)
	iocunditas (iudunditas)
	togorio (tugurio)
	exercito (exercitu)
inversely:	*territurio (territorio)*
	diabulus (diabolus)
	chaus (chaos)
o, ou, u often confused:	
	consolere (consulere)
	pictur (pictor)
u for *uu*:	*artum (artuum)*
u for *um:*	*per arbitriu (per arbitrium)*
uu for *u:*	*euuangelium (euangelium)*
u suppressed:	*ascultare (auscultare)*
inversely:	*protoplasti (protoplausti)*
u for *l:*	*cauculus (calculus)*

confusion of *-ulus, ellus*

confusion of *-aill- -alli-*

omission of an initial vowel:
lectuarium (electuarium)
conisma (iconisma)
xamitum (examitum)
in Spanis (in Hispanis)

Consonants:

b for *p:* *lebrosis (leprosis)*
recomposition: *obprobrium (opprobrium)*
b for consonantal *u:*
reuelabit (reuelauit)
deserbitor (deseruitor)
inversely: *suscitauit (suscitabit)*
freq. *c* for *ch:* *carta (charta)*
crisma (chrisma)
inversely: *chachinnus (cachinnus)*
Archadius (Arcadius)
charitas (caritas)
confusion between *-ci- and -ti-:*
saciaberis (satiaberis)
especially in suffixes:
ardenciorum (ardentiorem)
oracio (oratio)
deuocio (deuotio)
pernitiosus (perniciosus)
prouintia (prouincia)
cot for *quod*
c for *qu:* *secuntur (sequuntur)*
in the Middle Ages, *ch* for *h:*
michi (mihi)
nichil (nihil)
c suppressed after *x:*
exitare (excitare)
c suppressed before *t:*
cunti (cuncti)
inversely: *ancxietas (anxietas)*
c, k often confused:
calendarius (kalendarius)
karissimus (carissimus)
c for *sc:* *percindere (perscindere)*
cissor (scissor)
d for *t:* *inquid (inquit)*
capud (caput), adque (atque)
inversely: *aliut (aliud)*

aput (apud), CYPR.
am- for *adm-:* *amministro (administro)*
freq. *f* for *ph:* *freneticus (phreneticus)*
profeta (propheta)
fantasia (phantasia)
f for consonantal *u:*
efectus (euectus)
fiscum (viscum)
g for *c:* *negare (necare)*
giuitatem (ciuitatem)
g for *gu-* frequently
initial *h* suppressed:
asta (hasta)
ortabatur (hortabatur)
just as *h* at the beginning of a syllable:
aueunt (auehunt), GREG.-T.
initial *h* added: *habundare (abundare)*
hostiatim (ostiatim)
hac (ac)
some variants which can cause confusion:
ac or hac
hostium or ostium
hortus or ortus
h added in some Hebrew words:
Danihel (Daniel)
Bethlehem (Bethleem)
Ismahel (Ismael)
j (i) for *g:* *traiediam (tragediam)*
inversely *i* for *g*:
iniens (ingens)
ll for *l:* *mallens (malens)*
m for *n* before labial of a following word:
im peius (in peius)
final *m* added: *dummodom (dummodo)*
final *m* disappears in the declension (Vulgar Latin):
ceruolo facere (ceruulum facere)
mm for *m:* *consummat (consumat)*
m for *n:* *comsummatio (consummatio)*
n for *m* before *p* (recomposition):
inpeccantia (impeccantia)
n added: *gigans (gigas)*
uicinsimo (uicesimo)
succensu (successu)
(recomposition): *congnosci (cognosci)*
inversely *s* for *ns:*

cosul (consul)
p for *f* or *ph:* *piltris (filtris)*
p for *b:* *puplica (publica)*
optineo (obtineo)
p for *u:* *deseparo (deseuero)*
p for *ph:* *spera (sphaera)*
initial *p* suppressed:
thisana (ptisana)
sallentium (psallentium)
p developed between a labial and a dental:
columpna (columna)
sollempnitatem (sollemnitatem)
hiemps (hiems)
dampna (damna)
contempnunt (contemnunt)
temptare (tentare)
p suppressed between *r* and *t:*
absorti (absorpti)
p suppressed between *l* and *t:*
scultilis (sculptilis)
p for *pp:* *suplicium (supplicium)*
qu for *c:* *exquoquo (excoquo)*
q for *qu-* frequently in the Middle Ages:
ss for *sc* frequently in the Middle Ages:
s for *r:* *uideremus (var. uideremur),* GREG.-M., Ep. 9, 91; etc.
s for *c:* *seruisia (ceruisia)*
s suppressed in composition after *ex-:*
excindo (exscindo)
expecto (exspecto)
ss for *t:* *percussio (percutio)*
es- for *ex-* before a consonant:
especto (exspecto)
t and *th* confused:
Gothi or *Goti*
t for *d:* *rapitu (rapido)*
u for *b:* *aceruum (acerbum)*
t omitted: *uul (uult)*
w for *u:* *ewangelium (euangelium),* English
z for *di-:* *zabulus (diabolus)*
x for *ct:* *resurrexio (resurrectio)*
doubled consonants:
cappella (capella)
mississe (misisse)
Arrius (Arius)
lammina (lamina)

simplified consonants:

capa (cappa)
conexus (connexus)
cotidie (cottidie)
belua (bellua)

confusio of prefixes:

amitto (admitto)
admitto (amitto)
admouere (amouere)
diffinio (definio)

Appendix 2: Authors and Works cited*

Parentheses enclosing an abbreviation in full capitals, e.g. (SALL.), indicate a non-Christian writer. Latin names are given in parentheses after the English name. Abbreviations prefixed with 'PS.-' (PSEUDO-) are listed directly after the name of the real author.

Blaise uses his abbreviations casually, so many are not listed precisely in his 'Liste des auteurs et des ouvrages cités', but often a quick survey of the titles of a particular author will reveal the work Blaise has in mind. I have put in square backets, sometimes preceded by a question mark, works which are not precisely indicated by Blaise, although there are not many that are really questionable. Some abbreviations are not listed at all, and one can only conjecture; these appear at the end under 'Unlisted Abbreviations.'

For particular editions of works listed below the reader should consult Blaise's *Dictionnaire latin-français des auteurs chrétiens*, pp. 9-20. Most can be found in Migne's *Patrologia latina* (abbreviated M.) and *Patrologia graeca* (M.gr.), in the *Monumenta Germaniae historica* (MGH), and in the *Corpus scriptorum ecclesiasticorum latinorum* (CSEL). Newer editions, published after the *Dictionnaire*, can be found in the Corpus Christianorum series (Brepols). Blaise occasionally abbreviates the name of the editor without giving the name of the work, and he sometimes refers to authors in the original bibliography of the 1955 edition. The titles of works may vary from series to series, e.g. Augustine's *De actis cum Felice Manichaeo* in Migne's *Patrologia latina* becomes *Contra felicem libri duo* in the CSEL.

---

* [Appendix 2 is not included in Blaise's *Manuel* but has been compiled from his 'Liste des auteurs et des ouvrages cités' which appears in his *Dictionnaire latin-français des auteurs chrétiens*, pp. 9-20. The introductory paragraphs have been supplied by the translator.]

ACT. ARCHEL.	*Archelai episcopi liber disputationis aduersus Manichaeum* (5th c.), M.gr. 10	
ADAM.	Adamnan (Adamnanus or Adamanus), 9th abbot of the monastery of Iona (7th c.)	
AGAP. II	[? Agapetus II, Pope 946-56]	
ALCIM.	St. Avitus (Alcimus Ecdicius Auitus), bishop of Vienne, d. 518), M. 59	
AMBR.	St. Ambrose (Ambrosius), bishop of Milan (339-397)	
	Abr.	*De Abraham*
	Abrah.	[? *De Abraham*]
	Apol. Dau.	*Apologia prophetae Dauid*
	Bapt.	*De baptismo contra Donatistas*
	Bon. mort.	*De bono mortis*
	Cain et Ab.	[? *De Cain et Abel*]
	Ep.	*Epistulae*
	Hel.	*De Helia et ieiunio*
	Hex.	*Hexameron libri sex*
	In Psal.	[*Enarrationes in psalmos*]
	Iob et Dau.	[? *De interpellatione Iob et Dauid*]
	Nabuth.	[? *De Nabuthe*]
	Noe	*De Noe et arca*
	Obit. Th.	[? *De obitu Theodosii oratio*]
	Off.	*De officiis ministrorum*
	Parad.	*De paradiso*
	Psal. 118.	*Expositio psalmi XCVIII*
	Tob.	*De Tobia*
	Virg.	*De virginibus*
PS.-AMBR.	Pseudo-Ambrose	
	Serm.	*Sermones suppositi*
(AMM.)	Ammianus Marcellinus, historian (4th c.)	
ANAST.-BIBL.	[Anastasius Bibliothecarius (9th c.)]	
	Chronographia Tripertita, ed. Boor	
ANTON.	*Antonini Placentini Itinerarium*, an account of a pilgrimage to the holy places (6th c.)	
(APUL.)	Apuleius (2nd c.)	
ARN.	Arnobius (Arnobius) African rhetor (3rd or beg. 4th c.)	
	Disputationes aduersus nationes	
ARN.-I	Arnobius Junior (5th c.)	
	Ad Greg	[? *Liber ad Gregoriam in palatio constitutam*]
ARR. FRAG.	*Monumenta uetera ad Arianorum historiam pertinentia*, M.13, c. 557	
AVELLA.	*Auellana Collectio*, rescripts of emperors and Popes. CSEL, 35.	
AVG.	St. Augustine (Aurelius Augustinus), bishop of Hippo (354-430)	
	An. et or.	*De anima et eius origine*
	Beat. uit.	*De uita beata*

Breu. coll.	*Breuiculus collationis cum Donatistis*
Catech.	*De catechizandis rudibus*
C. Cresc.	[? *Contra Cresconium Donatistam*]
C. du. ep. Pelag.	*Contra duas epistulas Pelagianorum ad Bonifatium*
C. Fel.	[? *Contra Felicem*]
C. Faust.	[? *Contra Faustum Manichaeum*]
C. Gaud.	[? *Contra Gaudentium Donatistarum episcopum*]
Ciu.	*De ciuitate Dei*
C. Iul.	[? *Contra Iulianiam*]
C. Iul. op. imp.	*Contra secundam Iuliani responsionem imperfectum opus*
C. litt. Petil.	*Contra litteras Petiliani*
Coll. Don.	[? *Post collationem adversus Donatistas*]
Conf.	*Confessionum libri XIII*
C. part. Don.	[? *Psalmus contra partem Donati*]
Disc.	*De disciplina christiana*
Doct. chr.	*De doctrina christiana*
Emer.	*De gestis cum Emerino*
Enarr. psal.	[? *Enarratio in psalmos*]
Ep.	*Epistulae*
Ep. ad cath.	*Epistula ad catholicos*
Faust.	*Contra Faustum Manichaeum*
Frangip.	*[? = PS.-AVG., Serm. Frang. (Sermones a Frangipani monacho editi)]*
Gen. litt.	*De Genesi ad litteram*
Grat.	*De Gratia et libero arbitrio*
In Psal.	[? *Enarratio in psalmos*]
Locut.	[? *Locutionum in Heptateuchum libri septem*]
Mor. Manich.	[? *De moribus Manichaeorum*]
Nupt. et conc.	[? *De nuptiis et concupiscentia ad Valerium comitem*]
Ord.	*De ordine*
Parm.	*Contra epistulam Parmeniani*
Peccat. merit.	*De peccatorum meritis*
Peccat. orig.	[? *De peccato originali*]
Perf. iust.	[? *De perfectione iustitiae hominis*]
Post gest. Don.	[? *Post collationem aduersus Donatistas*]
Praedest.	*De praedestinatio sanctorum*
Psal.	*Enarratio in psalmos*
Qu. ad Simpl.	[? *De diuersis quaestionibus ad Simplicianum*]

	Serm.	*Sermones*
	Serm. (Mor.)	[? *Sermones post Maurinos reperti*, ed. Morin, Rome 1930]
	Spir. et litt.	*De spiritu et littera*
	Symb.	*De symbolo ad catechumenos*
	Tr. ep. Io.	[*In epistulam Iohannis ad Parthos tractatus*]
	Tr. eu. Io.	[? *In evangelium Iohannis tractatus*]
	Trin.	*De Trinitate*
	Vrb.	*De urbis excidio*
	Vnic. bapt.	*De unico baptismo*
	Vid.	*De bono uiduitatis*
PS.-AVG.	Pseudo-Augustine	
	C. Fulg. Don	[? *Contra Fulgentium Donatistam*]
	Hypomn.	*Hypomnesticon contra Pelagianos*
	Qu. test.	*Questiones ueteris et noui testamenti* (Ambrosiaster?)
	Serm.	[? *Sermones suppositi*]
	Serm. app.	*Sermones suppositi*
(A.-VICT.)	Aurelius Victor, historian (4th c.)	
(AVS.)	Ausonius, poet (4th c.)	
BACHIAR.	Bachiarius, Spanish monk (beg. 5th c.)	
	Repar. laps.	[? *De reparatione lapsi*]
BARNAB.	St. Barnabas, apostle	
	Ep.	*Barnabae uetus interpres*, epistula Graeca cum ueteri interpretatione latina
BED.	Venerable Bede (Venerabilis Beda), English monk (d. 735)	
	Hist.	*Historia ecclesiastica gentis Anglorum*
BEN	St. Benedict (Benedictus), patriarch of the monks of the West (beg. 6th c.)	
	Reg.	*Regula*
BONIF. I	Boniface I (Bonifatius), Pope (418-422)	
BON. II	[? BONIF. II]	
BONIF. II	Bonifatius II, Pope (530-32)	
	Epistulae	
(C.-AVR.)	Caelius Aurelianus, physician (5th c.)	
CAELEST. I	[? CAELESTIN.]	
CAELESTIN.	Celestine I (Caelestinus), Pope (422-432)	
	Ep.	*Epistulae*
CAES.-AREL.	St. Caesarius (Caesarius Arelatensis), bishop of Arles (d. 543)	
	Serm.	*Sermones*
	Serm. Mor.	[? *Sermones*, ed. Morin]
CASSIAN.	Cassian (Johannes Cassianus), monk in the East then at Marseilles, d. 435	
	Inst.	[? *De institutis coenobiorum et de octo principalium uitiorum re-mediis libri XII*]
	Coll.	*Collationes XXIV*

CASS.	Cassiodorus (Flauius Magnus Aurelius Cassiodorus Senator), d. approx. 583	
	Compl.	*Complexiones in epistulas apostolorum* (in *Acta et Apocalypsin*, M. 70)
	Hist.	[? *Historia ecclesiastica uocata tripertita*]
	Psal.	*Expositio in psalmos*
	Var.	*Variae*
(CATVL.)	Catullus (Catullus), poet, 1st c. B.C.	
(CIC.)	Cicero.	
	Fam.	[*Epistula ad familiares*]
	Fin.	[*De finibus*]
COMM.	Commodian (Commodianus), poet, end of 5th c.	
	Apol.	*Carmen apologeticum*
	Instr.	*Instructiones per litteras uersuum primas aduersus paganos*
CONC.	*Concilia*. See Mansi, *Sacrorum conciliorum noua et amplissima collectio*, Florentiae et Venetiis 1759-1798, 53 vols.	
CONC. CARTH. IV	[? *Concilia Carthaginiense*]	
CONC. MEROV.	*Concilia aeui Merouingici*, MGH Auct. ant. XII	
CONC. S.	*Acta Conciliorum Oecumenicorum*, ed. Schwartz, Berlin 1914+	
CORIPP.	Corippus (Flauius Cesconius Corippus), African bishop, poet (6th c.)	
	Io.	*Iohannes seu de bellis Libycis*
	Ioh.	[? *Iohannes seu de bellis Libycis*]
CYPR.	St.Cyprian (Thascius Caecilius Cyprianus), bishop of Carthage, d. 258.	
	Ad Demetr.	*Ad Demetrianum*
	Ad Don.	*Ad Donatum*
	Ad Fort.	*Ad Fortunatum de exhortatione martyrii*
	Bon. pat.	*De bono patientiae*
	Dom. orat.	*De Dominica oratione*
	Eccl. unit.	[? *De catholicae ecclesiae unitate*]
	Eccl. un.	[? *De catholicae ecclesiae unitate*]
	Ep.	*Epistulae*
	Hab. uirg.	*De habitu uirginum*
	Laps.	*De lapsis*
	Mort.	*De mortalitate*
	Op. et el.	*De opere et eleemosynis*
	Sent.	*Sententiae episcoporum de haereticis baptizandis*
	Sent. episc.	[? *Sententiae episcoporum de haereticis baptizandis*]
	Test.	*Ad Quirinum testimonia aduersus Iudaeos*
	Zel. et liu.	*De zelo et liuore.*
PS.-CYPR.	Pseudo-Cyprian	

	Aleat.	*De aleatoribus*
	De duod. abus.	[? *De duodecim abusiuis saeculi* (Irish author of the 7th c.)]
	Pasch. comp.	*De pascha computus*
	Rebapt.	*De rebaptismate*
	Sing.	*De singularitate clericorum*
	Sodom.	[? *Carmen Sodoma* or PS.-TERT.]
	Spect.	*De spectaculis* of Novatian, CSEL 23
DION.-EX.	Denys or Dionysius Exiguus (Dionysius Exiguus), Scythian monk who came to Rome, chronologist and translator (d. 545)	
ENNOD.	Ennodius (Magnus Felix Ennodius), bishop of Pavia (d. 521)	
	Ep.	*Epistulae*
	Op.	*Opuscula*
EVGIPP.	Eugippus (Eugippus), African monk, abbot in the region of Naples (5th c., 6th c.)	
	Ep.	*Epistula ad paschasium diaconum*
	Exc.	*Excerpta ex operibus S. Augustini*
	Seu.	[? *Vita S. Seuerini*]
	Vit. seu	[? *Vita S. Seuerini*]
	Vit.	[*Vita. S. Seuerini*]
FAUST.	[? FAUSTIN.]	
FAUSTIN.	Faustinus, Roman presbyter (4th c.)	
	Trin.	*De Trinitate, ad Gallam*
Placidam		
FAVST.-R.	Faustus of Riez (Faustus Rhegiensis or Reiensis), bishop of Riez (5th c.)	
	Spir. sc.	*De spiritu sancto*
FEL. II	Felix II, Pope (355-365)	
	Ep.	*Epistolae*
FILASTR.	St. Filaster, or Philaster (Filastrius), bishop of Brescia (end 4th c.)	
	Diuersarum haereseon liber	
FORT.	Venantius Fortunatus (Honorius Clementianus Venantius Fortunatus) (530-600), bishop of Poitiers, poet.	
	Carm.	*Carmina*
(FVLG.)	Fulgentius (Fabius Planciades Fulgentius), mythographer (5th c.)	
	Aet.	*De aetatibus mundi.*
GELAS.	Gelasius (Gelasius), Pope (492-496)	
	Ep.	*Epistulae*
	Tr.	*Tractatus*
GREG.-M.	St. Gregory the Great (Gregorius Magnus), Pope, b. approx. 540, Pope (590-604)	
	Dial.	*Dialogi*
	Ep.	*Epistulae*
	Hom.eu.	*In euangelia homiliae*
	Hom. Ez.	*In Ezechielem homiliae*
	Mor.	*Moralia in Job*
GREG.-T.	Gregory of Tours (Gregorius Turonensis), bishop of Tours (538-594)	

	Mart.	[? *Liber de passione et uirtutibus S. Iuliani martyris*]
	His.	*Historia Francorum*
	Hist.	[? *Historia Francorum*]
HADR. I	Hadrian (Hadrianus) I, Pope (772-795)	
	Epistolae	
HERM.	Hermas, Greek author (2nd c.)	
	Past.	*Pastor*
HIER.	St. Jerome (Sophronius Eusebius Hieronymus), b. approx. 347, d. 420	
	C. Pelag.	[? *Aduersus Pelagianos dialogi*]
	C. Ioan.	[*Adversus Ioannem Hierosolymitanum liber*]
	C. Lucif.	[? *Altercatio Luciferiani et orthodoxi seu dialogus contra Luciferianos*]
	Comm. psal.	[? *Commentarioli in psalmos*]
	C. Vigil.	[? *Aduersus Vigilantius liber*]
	Did. spir.	*Liber Didymi de Spiritu sancto, e Graeco*
	Ep.	*Epistulae*
	Ephes.	*Commentariorum in epistulam ad Ephesios libri III*
	Ez.	[? *Commentariorum in Ezechielem libri XVI*]
	Ez. hom.	[? perhaps *Homiliae XXVIII in Ieremiam et Ezechielem Graeco Origenis Latine redditae*]
	Gal.	*Commentariorum in epistulam ad Galatas libri III*
	Ier.	*Commentariorum in Ieremiam libri VI*
	In eccl.	[? *Commentarii in Ecclesiasten*]
	In Gal.	[? *Commentariorum in epistulam ad Galatas libri III*]
	In Ier.	[? *Commentariorum in Ieremiam libri VI*]
	In Is.	[? *Commentariorum in Isaiam libri XVIII*]
	Iou.	*Aduersus Iouinianum libri II*
	Is.	*Commentariorum in Isaiam libri XVIII*
	Matt.	*Commentariorum in Matthaeum libri IV*
	Orig. ez.	[? *Homiliae XXVIII in Ieremiam et Ezechielem Graeco Origenis Latine redditae*]
	Orig. luc. hom.	[? *In Lucam homiliae XXXIX ex Graeco Origenis Latine conuersae*]

	Pachom.	[? *Monitorium Pachomii uersio Latina* or *Regula S. Pachomi, e Graeco*]
	Pelag.	*Aduersus Pelagianos dialogi III*
	Qu. Hebr. Gen.	*Quaestionum Hebraicarum liber in Genesim*
	Tit.	*Commentariorum in epistulam Titum liber*
	Tr.	[? *Tractatus..., ed. Morin*]
	Tract.	[? *Tractatus...*]
	Tr. in Is.	[? *Tractatus in Isaiam*]
	Tr. in psal.	[? *Tractatus in psalmos...*]
	Tr. I in psal.	[? *Tractatus in psalmos, series prima*]
	Tr. II in psal.	[? *Tractatus in psalmos, altera series*]
	Tr. psal.	[? *Tractatus in psalmos*]
	Vit. Hil.	Vita S. Hilarionis eremitae
	Vir. ill.	De uiris illustribus liber
	Vit. Mal.	[? *Vita Malchi monachi*]
	Vit. Pauli	*Vita S. Pauli, primi eremitae*
PS.-HIER.	Pseudo-Jerome.	
HILAR.	St. Hilary (Hilarius Pictauiensis), bishop of Poitiers (b. approx. 315, bishop approx. 350, d. 367)	
	In Psal.	[*Tractatus super psalmos*]
	Mat.	*In euangelium Matthaei*
	Psal.	*Tractatus super psalmos*
	Trin.	*De trinitate*
HIPP.	Hippolytus of Rome, v. *La tradition apostolique*, ed. Dom Botte, Paris 1946	
(HOR.)	Horace, poet	
	Ep.	[? *Epistles*]
IGNAT.	*Ignatii epistula ad Romanos*, Old Latin translation	
INNOC.	Innocent I (Innocentius I), Pope (402-417)	
INTERP. IO.-CHRYS.	[Mutianus (6th c.), translator of St. John Chrysostum, M.gr. 63]	
	Hom.	[? *Homiliae*]
IORD.	Jordanes or Jordanis (Iordanes), Geat [in fact, a Goth], bishop of Ravenna (6th c.)	
	Get.	*De rebus Geticis*
IREN.	Translator of Irenaeus, a translation in Latin of St. Irenaeus, (b. in Asia, bishop of Lyons, 2nd. c.)	
	Peri haereseon	
ISID.	St. Isidore (Isidorus), bishop of Seville (b. approx. 560, d. 636)	
	Or.	[? *Originum libri*]
ITAL.	*Bibliorum sacrorum latinae uersiones antiquae seu uetus Italica*	
ITIN. BVRD.	*Itinerarium a Burdigala Hierusalem usque* (4th c.)	
IVVC.	Juuencus (Caius Vettius Aquilinus Iuuencus), Spanish presbyter, poet (4th c.)	
	Euang.	*De historia euangelica*
LACT.	Lactantius (Caecilius Firmianus Lactantius), African apologist (beg. of 4th c.)	
	Ep.	*Epitome diuinarum institutionum*

	Inst.	*Diuinarum institutionum libri VII*
	Opif.	*De opificio Dei*
LEO. M.	St. Leo the Great (Leo Magnus), Pope (440-461)	
	Serm.	*Sermones*
LEPTOG.	*Leptogenesis* (Small Genesis), a Latin translation of an apocraphyal part of the Old Testament, ed. Ceriani, *Monumenta sacra et profana*, 1861	
LIBER.	Liberius (Liberius), Pope (352-366).	
(LIV.)	Livy (Titus Liuius).	
LUCIAN.	Lucianus, correspondent of Cyprian (Ep. 22 and 22)	
LVCIF.	Lucifer Calaritanus, bishop of Caliari (d. approx. 371)	
	Athan.	*De sancto Athanasio libri duo*
	Non. Parc.	*De non parcendo in Deum delinquentibus*
	Moriend.	*Moriendum esse pro Dei Filio*
MAMERT.	Claudianus Mamertus, presbyter of Vienne in Gall (5th c.)	
	St. an.	*De statu animae*
MART.-BRAC.	Martin of Braga (Martinus Bracarensis), b. in Pannonia before 520, abbot then bishop of Dumio in Galicia in 556, archbishop of Braga (572-579)	
(M.-EMP.)	Marcellus Empiricus, physician (4th c.)	
(MINVC.)	Minucius Felix (Minucius Felix), end 2nd c.	
	Octauius	
MOZAR.	[? *Liber Mozarabicus sacramentorum*]	
NICET.	[? NICET.-R.]	
NICET.-R.	Nicetas, bishop of Remesiana in Dacia (d. after 414)	
	Spir.	*De Spiritus Sancti potentia*
OPTAT.	Optatus, bishop of Milevis in Numidia (4th c.)	
	Contra Parmenianum Donatistam	
OROS.	Orosius (Paulus Orosius), Spanish presbyter (5th c.)	
	Apol.	*Liber apologeticus*
	Hist.	*Historiarum aduersus paganos libri VII*
PACIAN.	Pacianus, bishop of Barcelona (d. before 392)	
	Ep.	*Epistula ad Symphorianum tertia*
P.-AQVIL.	Paulinus, patriarch of Aquileia (8th c.)	
	Ep.	*Epistulae*
PASS. AVR.	*Passio aureae* (6th c.)	
PASS. FRVCTVOSI	*Passio Fructuosi episcopi at soc.*	
PASS. ISAAC	[*Passio Maximiani et Isaac Donatistarum auctore Macrobio*, M. 8, c. 767]	
PASS. PERP.	*Passio SS. Perpetuae et Felicitatis* (3rd c.)	
PASS. VII MON.	[? PASS. VII. MONAC, v. PS.-VICT.-VIT.]	
PEREG.	*Peregrinatio ad loca sancta* (the author, incorrectly identified as Sylvia, sister of Rufinus of Aquitaine, is a Spanish woman, Etheria, or Egeria, who recounts her voyage to the East and to Jerusalem)	
PELAG.	Pelagius, translator of a Greek text, v. *Vitae Patrum*	
PETIL.	Petilianus, cp. AVG. *C. litt. Petil.*	
PETR.-CHRYS.	Petrus Chrysologus, archbishop of Ravenna (5th c.)	
	Serm.	*Sermones*

(PL.) Plautus
- *Trin.* — [*Trinummus*]

(PLIN.-I) Pliny the Younger

P.-NOL St. Paulinus (Meropius Pontius Paulinus Nolanus), bishop of Nola (353-431)
- *Carm.* — *Carmina*
- *Ep.* — *Epistulae*

P.-PELL. Paulinus of Pella (Paulinus Pellaeus), son-in-law of Ausonius
- *Euch.* — *Carmen quod inscribitur 'Eucharisticos Deo sub ephemeridis meae textu'*

P.-PETRIC. Paulinus of Perigueux (Paulinus Petricordiae), 5th c.
- *Mart.* — *De uita S. Martini episcopi*

PRVD. Prudentius (Aurelius Prudentius Clemens), poet (d. after 405)
- *Apoth.* — *Liber apotheosis*
- *Cath.* — *Liber cathemerinon*
- *Ham.* — *Hamartigeneia*

(QUINT.) Quintilian (1st c.)

RER. MEROV. *Scriptorum rerum Merouingicarum tomi VII* (MGH)

ROSSI (de) *Inscriptiones christianae Vrbis Romae* (Rome, 1857-88)

RVF. Rufinus (Tyrranius Rufinus), presbyter of Aquileia
- *Clem.* — *Clementis quae feruntur Recognitiones a Rufino translatae*
- *Greg. interp.* — [? see below]
- *Greg. orat.* — A translation of the apology and eight other works of Gregory Nazianzus, ed. Engelbrecht, CSEL
- *Hist. eccl.* — [? *Eusebii historia ecclesiastica a Rufino translata et continuata*]
- *Interp. Ios.* — [? = PS.-RVF, *Interp. Ios.* *(Flauii Josephi de Bello Iudaica versio latina)*]
- Orig. princ. — Origenis libri [περὶ ἀρχῶν] *seu de principiis libri IV*

PS.-RVF. Pseudo-Rufinus
- *In Am.* — *Commentarius in Amos prophetam*
- *Interp. Ios.* — *Flauii Iosephi de Bello Iudaico libri uersio latina* (v. Cass.)
- *Psal.* — *Commentarius in LXXV psalmos*

SACRAM. GELAS. *Sacramentarium Gelasianum*

SACRAM. GREG. *Sacramentarium Gregorium*

SACRAM. LEON *Sacramentarium Leonianum*

(SALL.) Sallust
- *Cat.* — [*Catalina*]

SALV. Salvian (Saluianus), presbyter of Marseilles (5th c.)
- *Eccl.* — *Ad ecclesiam*

	Gub.	*De gubernatione Dei*
(SEN.)	Seneca	
	Clem.	[*De Clementia*]
SEDVL.	Caelius Sedulius, presbyter (5th c.)	
	Carm. pasch.	*Carmen Paschale*
	Op.	*Opus Paschale*
SEPT.	Septuagint	
SERM. ARR. FRAG.	[? *Sermonum Arrianorum fragmentum series prima*]	
SID.	St. Sidonius Apollinaris (C. Sollius Sidonius Apollinaris), bishop of Clermont (5th c.).	
	Ep.	*Epistulae*
SOCR.	[Socrates Scholasticus, *Historia Ecclesiastica*, M.gr. 67]	
(SOPH.)	Sophocles	
(SPART.)	Spartian, historian (4th c.)	
STEPH. II	Stephanus II, Pope (8th c.)	
SVLP.-SEV.	Sulpicius Severus (Sulpicius Seuerus), end 4th c.	
	Mart.	*De vita beati Martini liber unus*
	Chron.	*Chronicorum libri duo*
	Dial.	*Dialogi*
SYMM.	Symmachus, Pope (5th c.)	
	Ep.	*Epistulae*
(TAC.)	Tacitus	
TERT.	Tertullian (Quintus Septimius Florens Tertullianus), beg. 3rd c.	
	An.	*De anima*
	Ad mart.	*Ad martyras*
	Adu. Marc.	[? *Aduersus Marcionem*]
	Apol.	*Apologeticus*
	Bapt.	*De baptismo*
	Carn. Chr.	*De carne Christi*
	Cast.	*De exhortatione castitatis*
	Cor.	*De corona*
	Cult. fem.	*De cultu feminarum*
	Herm.	*Aduersus Hermogenum*
	Idol.	*De idoloatria*
	Iei.	*De ieiunio aduersus Psychicos*
	Marc.	*Aduersus Marcionem*
	Monog.	[? *De monogamia*]
	Nat.	*Ad nationes*
	Orat.	[? *De oratione*]
	Paen.	*De paenitentia*
	Pall.	*De pallio*
	Pat.	*De patientia*
	Praescr.	*De praescriptione haereticorum*
	Prax.	*Aduersus Praxean*
	Pud.	*De pudicitia*
	Res.	*De resurrectione carnis*
	Scorp.	*Scorpiace*
	Spect.	*De spectaculis*
	Val.	*Aduersus Valentinianos*
	Virg. uel.	[? *De uirginibus uelandis*]
	Vx.	*Ad uxorem*
THEOD.	Theodosius (6th c.)	
	Sit.	*De situ terrae sanctae*

THEOD.-MOP. Theodore, bishop of Mopsuestia (5th c.)
- *Col.* — Latin version of a commentary on the Epistle to the Colossians
- *In ep. ad Phil.* — [?]
- *In Gal.* — *Commentarius in epistulas Petri ad Galatas*

(TREB.) Trebellius Pollio, historian (4th c.)

VEREC. Verecundus, bishop in Africa (6th c.)
- *Cant.* — *Commentarius super cantica ecclesiastica*
- *Cant. Eccl.* — [? *Commentarius super cantica ecclesiastica*]

VICT. Claudius Marius Victor (Claudius Marius Victor), rhetor at Marseilles (5th s.)
- *Aleth.* — *Alethia*
- *Verb. script.* — *De uerbis scripturae: factum est uespere et mane* (PS.-MAR.-VICT.)

VICT.-POETOV. St. Victorinus (Victorinus Petauionensis or Poetouionensis), bishop of Pettau in Pannonia (d. 304)

VICT.-VIT. Victor Vitensis (Victor Vitensis), bishop of Vita in Africa (5th c.)
- *Historia persecutionis Vandalicae*

(VIRG.) Virgil

VIT. PATR. *Vitae Patrum*, M. 73-74

(VLP.) Ulpian, jurisconsult (2nd c.)

(VOP.) Vopiscus, historian (4th c.)

VVLG. The Vulgate (Vulgata)

VETUS TESTAMENTUM

Dan.	*Daniel*
Deut.	*Deuteronomium*
Eccli.	*Ecclesiasticus*
Esdr.	*Esdras I, II, III, IV*
Ex.	*Exodus*
Ez.	*Ezechiel*
Gen.	*Genesis*
Ier.	*Ieremias*
Ier. Iam.	[*Lamentationes Ieremiae prophetae*]
Ios.	*Iosue*
Is.	*Isaias*
Iud.	*Iudices*
Leu.	*Leuiticus*
Mich.	*Michaeus*
Num.	*Numeri*
Par.	*Paralipomena*
Prou.	*Prouerbia Salomonis*
Ps.	*Psalmi*
Reg.	*Reges*
Sap.	*Sapientia*
Tob.	*Tobias*

Zach.	*Zacharias*

NOUUM TESTAMENTUM

Act.	*Actus apostolorum*
Apoc.	*Acopalypsis*
Col.	*Pauli epistula ad Collossenses*
Cor.	*Pauli epistulae ad Corinthios*
Gal.	*Pauli epistula ad Galatas*
Hebr.	*Pauli epistula ad Hebraeos*
Iac.	*Epistula Iacobi*
Io.	*Euangelium Ioannis*
Io. ep.	*Iohannis epistulae*
Luc.	*Euangelium Lucae*
Marc.	*Euangelium Marci*
Mat.	*Euangelium Matthaei*
Petr.	*Epistulae Petri*
Philipp.	*Pauli epistula ad Philippenses*
Rom.	*Pauli epistula ad Romanos*
Thess.	*Pauli epistulae ad Thessalonicenses*
Tim.	*Pauli epistulae ad Timotheum*

UNLISTED ABBREVIATIONS (numbers refer to pages of this translation)

TRACT. DE DIVIT. (12)	[?]
AMBR. *Sacram.* (17)	[? *De Sacramentis*]
CYPR. *Orat.* (24)	[? *De Dominica oratione*]
PASS. RVF. (68)	[? *Passio Rufinus*]
PASS. BON. ET MAX. (82)	[? *Passio Bonifatii et Maximi*]
PASS. XII AFR. (110)	[?]

Index

Numbers refer to sections (§).